regretsy

regretsy

Where DIY Meets WTF

April Winchell

 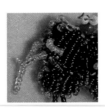  

Villard
New York

A Villard Books Trade Paperback Original

Copyright © 2010 by April Winchell

Published in the United States by Villard Books,
an imprint of The Random House Publishing Group,
a division of Random House, Inc., New York.

VILLARD BOOKS and VILLARD & "V" CIRCLED Design
are registered trademarks of Random House, Inc.

The term "Etsy" is a trademark of Etsy, Inc. This book
is not affiliated with Etsy, Inc.

Photo credits can be found on pages 155–157.

ISBN 978-0-345-52318-1

Printed in the United States of America on acid-free
paper

www.villard.com

9 8 7 6 5 4 3 2 1

contents

introduction

It all started with a Barack Obama rug.

A shitty white kitchen rug, with a terrible portrait of Barack Obama stenciled on it. And it came postage due.

This was starting to become kind of a thing with my friends Drew and Scott. They routinely sent me ugly crap they found on Etsy, as sort of an endless white elephant gift exchange. Except I wasn't exchanging anything. I was keeping all of it.

To understand this game a little better—and to understand Regretsy, for that matter—you have to know that I am completely fascinated by self-expression that misses the mark in some way. Sure, I love bad singing and wooden acting as much as the next guy, but it's not just poorly executed work that delights me.

For example, I have a beautifully painted oil on velvet of Phil Spector in my bedroom. The artwork is technically proficient, but what the fuck is going on there? Who would be moved to paint Phil Spector, sitting in the courtroom with his giant fro, on trial for murder? That's the question I ask myself. I already know who would buy it.

This unnatural appetite has carried over into my professional life with a vengeance. Before Regretsy, I had a radio show in Los Angeles for several years. I devoted much of my airtime to Zsa Zsa Gabor rapping and torturous spoken-word performances by Leonard Nimoy. The highlight of those years was a two-hour interview with Pat Boone, during which I managed to play his entire heavy-metal CD. And my favorite remote was at the ninety-nine-cent store on Halloween, treating listeners to a dollar wine tasting.

So when I discovered Etsy in 2007, it was like I'd died and went to

Hemet. Sure, there were thousands of beautiful pieces for sale, but for every flawless handcraft, there was a pot holder made of upcycled sweatpants.

And ultimately, that's what got me hooked. Everything I loved was in there somewhere: the bizarre, the misguided, and the unintentionally hilarious. I just had to find it. It was the same thrill of the hunt as someone with more refined tastes, only in reverse. I was picking through pearls, looking for shells.

Of course, it's not enough for a piece to be bad. It has to have something special to go from a piece of crap to a piece of crap I've got to have. And while that's largely an intangible, there are a few things I tend to look for.

First, it has to be genuine. As with any comedy, the piece cannot be played for laughs. There has to be a sincerity to it, a lack of awareness that gives it charm.

Second, it has to be asking for my derision in some way, because that's the mitigating factor that allows me to be an asshole. The piece can be overpriced, poorly made, or something no one but the artist will ever understand. Or it might be a completely ordinary piece, sick with love for itself (or as I call it, "up its own ass"). This results in labored exposition, long diatribes about inspiration, allusions to classical works, and detailed accounts of the emotional journey during the creation of the object, which is usually ugly as hell. Bonus points if any of this is in verse.

So naturally, as I unearthed the ridiculous wine bottle lamps and glittering tampon cozies, I shared these treasures with like-minded friends, spreading the glow of mediocrity. And Scott and Drew were only too happy to play along. In fact, they began to follow up every get-together with some terrible object, which came in the mail under the guise of a thank-you gift.

One fateful day, I came home to a missed delivery notice on my door from the postman. He had been trying to deliver a package from South Africa addressed to Miss Bunny Schlemmerkindman (an inside joke among the three of us). It was all very funny until I had to go down to the post office and try to claim it with no ID in that name, postage due, from South Africa, with customs tax. By the time I got home, I was a little cranky.

And then I opened it.

On May 23, 2009, at 10:33 AM, April Winchell wrote: THE EAGLE HAS LANDED. I got the rug, and may I say, it's even more hideous than I imagined.

On May 23, 2009, at 10:44 AM, Drew O'Brien wrote: I'm sorry this has turned out to be such an ordeal. My regrEtsy!!

On May 23, 2009, at 10:56 AM, April Winchell wrote: REGRETSY!!! That is fucking HILARIOUS. I am going to register that domain RIGHT NOW.

And I did. And then I forgot about the whole thing.

In September, while cleaning out my email folder, I found the confirmation for the domain and decided to just go for it. I figured I'd stockpile a week or two of posts and just come out swinging. I didn't think Etsy would even hear about it for a while, and by then I would have at least had some fun.

On October 1, Regretsy went live with no advertising, no fanfare and no money. A few hours later, I was buying a coffeemaker when I got a text from my friend Gina, telling me Regretsy was on the front page of Buzzfeed and was going viral.

I'd like to say that this was all a result of my incredible marketing savvy, and I'll admit, I did do a few things right. For example, I decided to do the site under the name "Helen Killer," because I thought not knowing who was behind it would make it more interesting (I also thought I'd get more valuable feedback if people were focused on the site and not the person writing it).

But between you and me and my mother, who is the other person reading this book, Regretsy is a textbook case of dumb luck. So much was going on I didn't know about and could never have planned.

For one thing, crafting was much bigger than I'd thought, which meant that my potential audience was, too. And not just crafters themselves, but people who liked handcrafts, as well as people who hated them. Then there's the whole "Brooklyn hipster" sort of vibe to the homemade movement, which people either love or love to hate. And of course, snark itself has become more and more popular in recent years, so Regretsy is a treasure trove for fail fans.

I also zeroed in directly on Etsy, which turned out to be incredibly fortuitous. Etsy has a very strict commenting policy and will shut down any thread that "calls out" a seller, meaning that sniping about other people's work isn't permitted. This climate of censorship had created a rising bubble of discontent. As usual, I was the prick.

Within twenty-four hours, Regretsy had over 1.3 million hits. I was absolutely dumbfounded. I was getting hundreds of emails and tweets, with thousands of people joining my Facebook page and following me on Twitter. I already had something of a profile on the Internet, but I was quickly eclipsing my own fan base, proving that Regretsy was now more popular than I was.

For about three days, I sat in bed at my laptop, just trying to keep up. Everyone started picking up on it, from Gawker to Gizmodo, followed by *The Wall Street Journal*, which covered it twice in two weeks. Then came one national newspaper after another, and even the BBC. Within two weeks I had cracked the top five thousand sites in the United States and had an offer to buy the site and interest from multiple literary agencies. I never saw it coming.

Needless to say, all of this attention and success created a lot of discussion. A popular theory on Twitter was that Regretsy was the work of Diablo Cody. Word on the Etsy forums was that Regretsy was created by a disgruntled Etsy seller, or maybe even by Etsy itself (but since Regretsy is critical of Etsy sellers, these threads were quickly closed down).

A few days later, someone sent me a link to a thread where Etsy sellers were complaining about my *not* linking back to them. This really stunned me, because I never imagined there would be any value in doing that. But God love them, they knew more than I did. Which, by the way, is not difficult to do.

Obviously, this changed everything. Because when I started linking, the featured listings started selling. And when I saw that Regretsy could actually be a powerful selling tool for these kinds of pieces, my entire focus changed. Or more accurately, I got a focus.

Suddenly the site wasn't just something to do for my own amusement. It wasn't just about snarking on things I thought were ridiculous or strange anymore; it had a purpose. It was now a place where products end up being "promoted," albeit in a completely backward and unexpected way, and that made it into something really exciting.

When you make coats for farm animals or wall art with masturbating dinosaurs, people aren't going to find you with a keyword search. Unless you make a very specific sort of product that supports the aesthetic Etsy has so successfully created, you're really invisible. Its unlikely you'll wind up on the front page with a cheese-grater clock, or a vampire doll with bloody teeth for eyes. Unusual and unconventional products sometimes find their audience in unusual ways. And to my great surprise and delight, this is often what Regretsy has been able to bring about.

As of this writing, Regretsy has been indirectly responsible for the sale of hundreds of pieces, and, by my calculations, has sent millions of hits to Etsy stores. Every day I get emails from people I've never featured, asking why they have ten, twenty, fifty, even one hundred referral visits from Regretsy. I explain to them that when someone clicks over from Regretsy to see a featured piece, they frequently go shopping, which results in many stores getting new traffic and many sales that would never have happened otherwise. The idea that so much positive comes from something so negative is redeeming for me. The sales and positive experiences that sellers enjoy as a result of being featured on Regretsy reduce my asshole footprint.

And I've also learned a lot about myself, and my own ego. The truth is, I'm having much the same experience as the people I feature. I never thought I would find my audience this way. I never thought this would be the book I'd write. But does it really matter? Does William Shatner refuse his paychecks because he isn't getting the same job offers as Robert De Niro? Does Thomas Kinkade turn down licensing deals because he thinks he belongs in the Louvre? Are the Olsen twins giving back the millions they made on shitty clothes for tweens because they'd rather be Dolce & Gabbana?

There is great grace in accepting blessings that come in unexpected ways, and the sellers in this book have taught me that many times over. We should all aspire to having such humor and insight.

At the end of the day, every artist needs to be seen. It's less important how the public finds you than that they do find you.

Thank you for finding me, and the people in this book.

regretsy

& Accessories

I'll admit it: I'm not as whimsical as I used to be.

And I used to be plenty whimsical, believe me. I had a messenger bag made out of a welcome mat. I had two pairs of the same pumps in different colors, and often wore one of each. I wore a hat made out of a paper bag. Really, I was one step away from clown college.

These days, I just don't have the energy for that kind of shit. Maybe it's a function of aging, but I find myself much less willing to tie birds to my head or wear giant felt pins that look like breakfast foods. So it's kind of a shame that Etsy came into existence as I was already growing out of that stuff, because it truly is the clearinghouse for whimsical fuckery.

As of this writing, a search of Etsy's handmade category brings up more than 33,000 items tagged "whimsical." That's an assload of whimsy. Parenthetically, there are more than 100 items tagged "whimsicle," but that's more sad than funny.

Whimsy, insofar as jewelry and accessories are concerned, seems to mean one of two things: either the proportions are wrong, or the object is made with unexpected materials. Proportional whimsy could mean a twelve-foot scarf or a cowl that obscures your entire head, or, conversely, it could mean an extremely tiny hat. Whimsical materials could mean a necklace of teddy bear heads or a trench coat made of attic insulation. It is important to note, however, that whimsy is not the same as upcycling, which is basically taking garbage and making something useless out of it.

It might seem like a lot now, but at one point in my life, 1,600 pages of whimsy would have been a tease. I couldn't get enough of that smirking, winking fabulousness. I loved the theatricality of it all: necklaces made from Formica samples, vintage men's pajamas as outerwear, piles of costume jewelry from obsessive thrift store scavenging. I adored my rhinestone-studded cigarette holder, my fingerless gloves, my neon socks, my Mary Janes with kitten faces on them. I basked in the wholly unwarranted confidence that anything looked great if you meant it.

And it's true that attitude does go a long way. But as with any road trip, there are markers in the road that keep you from drifting out of your lane and into oblivion. And I distinctly recall a moment in my mid-twenties when I first heard the sound of driving over them.

I was working as a receptionist in a law firm, and I had become friendly with the office manager. Beth was an older woman with a son in high school, and he had developed an interest in acting. While I wasn't pursuing it at the time, it was common knowledge that my mother and father were in the business, and that I had worked as a child actress for a number of years.

Beth came by my desk one morning and asked what I was doing that weekend. For reasons I still don't understand, I said, "Nothing," then watched in abject horror as she dropped two tickets to her son's high school production of *The Crucible* on my desk. I started to demur, but she quickly said, "Oh, they're free." And, leaning closer, she whispered, "Industry comps."

I quickly called my friend Debi, who, like me, heard "industry comps" first, "*Crucible*" second, and "high school" not at all. We arranged to meet at her house several hours before the show, so we'd have enough time to get ready.

It was late October, so this event called for a fall wardrobe. I packed up all my sweaters and leggings—despite the fact that it was in the mid-seventies in the valley—and drove to her house with the air-conditioning on full blast.

Anticipating my arrival, Debi had already laid out her entire wardrobe on the bed and stolen a pack of her mother's Parliaments. We began the arduous task of making it work, and if this had been a John Hughes movie, this is where the montage would have gone.

Debi settled on a green wraparound Danskin dress and an enormous antebellum hat, which is always a good choice for theater-going. I chose a knee-length zebra sweater with purple spandex leggings and bright orange platforms. And as we left the house, lingering in the mirrored foyer of her mother's condo, we felt every bit as fabulous as we were convinced we looked.

The first half of the play was horrible though uneventful. No one even complained about Debi's hat (though I realize now that the people behind us were probably grateful for the distraction). As the lights came up for intermission, Debi and I went outside to smoke and look important.

We were standing in the courtyard, trying to figure out how we could leave early without Beth hearing about it, when I noticed two women staring at us. They weren't even talking, really, just staring. It suddenly occurred to me that they must have heard us pick up our "industry comps" at will-call and were trying to figure out who we were! I was about to share this theory with Debi when one of the ladies suddenly turned to her friend and said, "Oh that's right, it's *tomorrow.*"

It took a second or two before I realized that it was October 30.

Aerial Photo

Mermaid Hair Clip

$54.00

Description

I never answer.
and she always wonder if that funny knot hurts.
so she sits,
especially in the evening
when cream and ribbons smells alike.

If I had to wear a Barbie doll and two pounds of broken jewelry on my head, I wouldn't be happy, either. But for God's sake, at least *try* to smile. This looks like a hostage photo at the Mattel plant.

Logjam

Birch Bark Purse – very unique, one of a kind (OOAK) special occasion hand bag

$75.00

"Special occasion"? What kind of special occasion? A lumberjack wedding? I don't know about you, but I don't have the coordination to hold a log and a drink at the same time. How about we just put this in the fireplace and call it Christmas?

Party Platter

RITZY in BLACK – cocktail ring – 2.75 inch CERAMIC

$47.00

Description

Make a huge statement with this bold ceramic cocktail ring. It has a diameter of 6.5 centimetres and is adorned with feathers and tiny beads which create an elegant cuff over the hand.

Be the envy of all.

It's called a "cocktail ring" because you can balance a twelve-ounce tumbler on it. And it's ceramic, so you're all set when the hot hors d'oeuvres come out.

Perfectly Charmin

Astrid Spats

$80.00

Description

Whether it be a wedding, a summer stroll, or even (yes!) to work, wherever you choose to wear these babies, you will be noticed.

If you really want to be noticed, try crapping your pants on the bus. It might not be ironic, but it's less embarrassing than wearing yellow spats to (yes!) work.

Semi-Colon

Brooch with Vintage Buttons

$22.00

Description

Two vintage celluloid buttons were stacked and adhered with epoxy to create this spiffy brooch. Two layers of black wool felt have been hand sewn to the back along with a silver plated brooch clasp. Pin them on a jacket, coat, hat or purse for a swell look!

Tell her you'd marry her all over again with a prolapsed anus.

Cereal Killer

Golden Cheerio

$ 5.25

Hand burnished with gold leaf then dipped in a bath of clear resin, strung on a gorgeous 18" sterling silver ball strand chain.

Please do not eat this cheerio.

Free first class shipping.

Stays elegant, even in milk!

Bird Brain

Crimson Bliss

$40.00

Description

black satin headband with a sheer burgundy bow, a vintage style gold and white charm and a 6" white dove

---

So, let's see. There's a black satin headband, and a burgundy bow, and a gold and white charm, and what else . . . what else . . . oh yeah, **A GIANT FUCKING BIRD GLUED TO YOUR HEAD**

Looking Sharp

Coca Cola Bottlecap Fun Earrings for women
by Justine Justine

$10.00

Description

Recycled!
Upcycled!
whatever you call it, i love it! its eco-friendly and funky!
these bottlecap-earrings are made with love and dedication in Mexico

Tetanus shots not included.

Wing It

BUTTERFLY BROOCH xxx It is whimsical xxx HANDCRAFTED xxx HANDBEADED

$14.99

Description

This little brooch wants to go have fun with you.

It also wants to look like a butterfly. But that isn't going to happen, either.

Cold Stone Fox

Ice cream headache headband

$20.00

Description

This Ice Cream Headache headband is surprisingly light on the head, as the creamy delicacies are purely paper pulp!

Hilarity ensues as people ask "what's that on your head?"

And you say, "It's a headband with a plastic dish full of fake paper ice cream glued to it!"

And they say, "Did you make that?"

And you say, "No, I bought it for twenty dollars."

And that's when everybody starts laughing.

Scum and Get It

Charming Pond Scum Amoeba Pendant

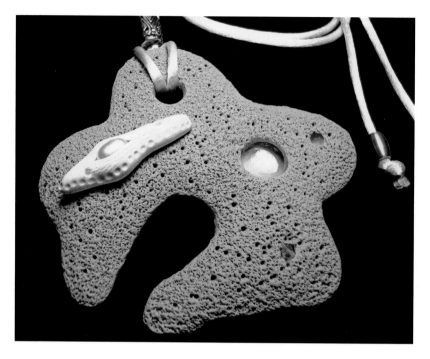

$39.95

Description

This charming pond scum green amoeba pendant features a beautiful clear contractile vacuole. This amoeba is voracious, as you can see by the six highly developed pseudopods.

If you would like to purchase the matching earrings, just Convo me and I'll make a separate listing for two small amoeba, one large one and a dear little paramecium.

"Your pond scum is lovely!"

"Really? Do you think so?"

"I do! Normally I don't go in for unicellular ciliate protozoa, but that's just got *Eukaryota* written all over it."

"What a relief! I thought it might be clashing with my blepharisma!"

I'd Rather Have a Bottle in Front of Me

Glow in the dark zombie brain cameo

$12.00

Description

Glow in the dark brain on a brass cameo. Cameo comes on an 18 inch brass colored necklace with lobster claw clasp. Cameo measures 1 inch high and .75 inches wide.

It glows in the dark to remind you how stupid it is.

Beaded Seat Cover

Still Life Panties

$350.00

Description

These are upcycled panties painted with a still life of flowers in a vase on my kitchen table. they are intended to be displayed clothes pined to a clothing line. ill include some twine and two clothes pins and you do the rest. they are double sided so if you want to change things up simply flip them over!

I bought a pair of these once. Oh, they were pretty, but I don't recommend wearing them to spin class.

Lunatic Fringe

Tassel and Studs Chic Shades

$25.00

Description

These are lots of fun. I added tassels and studs to the frame of this cool shades. The lens measures 2 inches. The glasses have UV protection. Maximum coverage. Never been worn. Or (Give a gift from the heart)

Oh, these are useful. Glasses you can't see through. Now all I need are a pair of lace spats and a sweater with no neck hole.

Lame Chop

Lamb Chop Headband

$15.00

Description

This is a wide band covered in a red/ multi colored dot satin and adorned with a plastic lamb chop, and floral brussel sprout, mushroom, pepper, and garnish leaf.

Finish your headband! There are children in China with no bobby pins!

Tiny tree earring ladder

$15.00

Description

This sweet little twig ladder is perfect for displaying 3 pair of earrings or any other small dangling items. The twigs are bound with leather and securely mounted on wood.

Perfect for the Eskimo woman with an earring collection, or for drying small strips of rabbit meat.

REGRETSY

QUEEN

PET HUMILIATION

I've had dogs my whole life. I grew up with German shepherds, Chihuahuas, Dalmatians, and a rotating cast of unplanned litters that my sisters and I would bring home to Mom, leaving her to find permanent homes for them.

As the years went on, my family adopted collies, Great Danes, Irish setters, and Westies. I've fostered Samoyeds and retrievers. And in the last twenty years, I've personally owned three pit bulls, a wire fox terrier, and a Boston.

I've discovered that even with so many different breeds and disparate temperaments, all dogs can be neatly divided into two categories: dogs who will let you put clothes on them, and dogs who will not.

Dogs who allow it do so for one reason only: *to make you happy.* That's it. Fans of dressing animals often insist that the pet "enjoys it," but this is, in fact, a terrible lie. Dogs do not appreciate having to take a crap in harem pants. They don't have favorite football teams or political leanings. And if left to their own devices, dogs almost never wear vests, unless you're talking about cartoons, in which case they still don't wear pants.

No, this kind of thing is all about you. Your dog doesn't care about being hot. She doesn't need fragrance to feel more feminine and she doesn't want to look like Lil' Kim. It's also unnecessary to dress her in a bridal gown when you breed her. Your dog is not a whore, and she's not a bride. She's a dog, and she'd rather eat her own shit than get her nails painted.

Oh, I suppose you might have an argument when it comes to weather-related garments, but even that's somewhat suspect. If your dog is going to be so cold that he needs a Russian Cossack hat and fur-lined waders, maybe you should bring him in the damn house.

At this point, you might be wondering what gives me the right to speak with such authority on this subject. Who the hell am I, anyway? Well, I'll tell you who I am. I am someone who has looked into the face of pet humiliation and seen my own reflection in its cold, wet nose.

I have a wire fox terrier named Mac. Wires have strange, coarse coats that don't shed. Breeders recommended that you "strip" them, meaning you have to actually pluck out the dead hair with your fingers.

Everywhere.

When I first read this in a wire fox terrier book, I was horrified. I couldn't imagine pulling all of her hair out. But the book stressed that this isn't painful for the dog, and, in fact, they can grow to like it. The author related her experience of sitting in front of the TV with her dog on her lap, pulling little tufts of hair out while the dog slept comfortably. So I thought I would give it a try.

It wasn't good. It probably wasn't painful, but Mac was not enjoying it. After every little pull, she would crane her head around and stare at me with wet eyes, imploring me to take up needlepoint.

I thought about doing this to her entire body, between her little toes and around her mouth and eyes, and finally I just said, Fuck it—if shaving is good enough for me, it's good enough for her.

I soon discovered that while shaving is easier, it presents a whole new problem: the dog slowly loses its color. Stripping is the only method that allows them to keep their distinctive brown heads.

I was in denial. I checked her after every shaving, and comforted myself that the color was still there. This may happen to other dogs, but not Mac, I told myself.

And then, almost overnight, I was confronted with the inevitable. My golden girl had become an oatmeal, dishwater head. This bothered me more than I expected. In fact, it bothered me almost every time I looked at her. And so I crossed the line.

I decided to try to fix it. Not for me, of course, *but for her.* Because surely, when she sees her reflection in the toilet bowl, she must wonder, "Is this all there is? Did I fritter away my youth foolishly pursuing the ball under the couch? Should I have been more interested in the world I'll leave behind than licking my own ass?"

And so I started researching ways to restore her color. I figured they dye dogs for shows, so there must be some kind of color I could use to make her feel young and beautiful again.

I finally settled on a particular type of henna product that doesn't have metallic salts in it, or peroxide, ammonia, or any other harsh chemicals. In fact, this stuff is so pure you can actually eat it, though I don't recommend it, unless your only other choice is the Olive Garden.

I went out onto the patio with Mac, and we sat in the sunshine while I carefully applied henna to her head. I coated her whiskers with petroleum jelly so there would be no bleed on her white beard, and combed the mud through her face and ears.

After the proper time had passed, I lovingly shampooed her (something she actually enjoys). The whole process was very pleasant for both of us.

Until her hair dried.

She looked like a cheese puff. Her entire head was a neon orange that would only get brighter with subsequent shampoos. And since these dogs don't shed, the color lasted through the holidays, giving many the ample opportunity to point and laugh. And each time, I knew it was my vanity and weakness that had brought that shame upon her.

Whenever people ask, "Don't you wish your dog could talk?" I think about Mac moping around the house, looking like Lucy after Ricky tells her she can't be in the show, and I have to answer no. She would no doubt bring it up over and over again, and would probably give me that whole Joe Pesci speech about how she isn't just a clown, here to amuse me.

Though if she could talk, I think she would sound more like Deborah Kerr.

Kentucky Frilled Chicken

Chicken Poncho or Knitted Wrist Cuff

$15.00

Description

This isn't a joke.

This poncho/human wrist cuff is being modeled by Bantam Chick Lil Dayna. I made it specifically for her. She's so beautiful – even more so than her nine sisters. I'm making ponchos and shrugs for them too.

"Some folks say that on a cold night, when the moon is a-howlin', you can still see her at the old farmhouse table, knitting shrugs for the chickens."

Kung Fou Fou

Snowflake basset outfit

$25.00

Description

Sparkly blue snowflake fabric makes this a holiday favorite for boys. Wrap coat style coat and comes with a cute pompom hat.

"I cannot see, Grasshopper, but if I could, I would surely kill you."

Table for Two

Double Feeder Hummingbird Hat

$37.00

Also works with dogs, though the pork chops can get heavy.

Bear dog outfit

$29.99

Description

Cute fleece bear face bodice, is attached to a pink rufflly skirt, The bear has an adorable pom pom nose, and come with matching bear hair bow.

The poor thing is sticking her tongue out at you. That's all she can do; there's a three-day waiting period on handguns.

Pamper Your Cat

Dirty Diaper cat toy

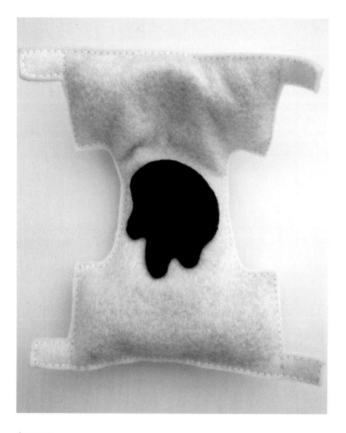

$9.00

Description

Oh NO! look what kitty is playing with!
It's a Poopy Diaper, and kitty can't stop smelling it!
Each one is stuffed to capacity with Super Strong 100% Organic Catnip
that will send your cat to the Moon.
No Filler!

Stoned out of your mind with a dirty diaper. Sounds like Richard
Branson in ten years.

PINK LEOPARD GOAT COAT

$29.99

You know what goats like? They like grass. They like tin cans. They like going behind the shed and taking a shit in peace. They don't like having leopard outfits strapped to their sagging haunches like Kim Cattrall.

If you absolutely have to put clothes on your goat, at least be humane enough to eat the fucking thing afterward so it doesn't have to live with the memory.

Many years ago, when we were still capable of being entertained by things that didn't involve vampires, my father made a pretty good living as a ventriloquist. He was very serious about his craft, and even made his own puppets. They were complicated things, with lots of levers and intricate mechanisms. Some even had special abilities, like blowing smoke out of their ears or spitting water.

My dad constructed everything by hand, including their sawdust-stuffed bodies, which were sewn to wooden frames. He carefully made their heads with layers of fiberglass and painted their features with little bottles of enamel paint. He even made their clothes by cutting down boys' suits and sewing slits in the backs of the jackets so he could reach in and work their heads.

So you might think that, growing up in this kind of environment, I would be able to make a simple felt doll. And yet you would be wrong. Terribly, terribly wrong.

I started trying to make toys a few years ago, and I think I've proven conclusively that handiness is not genetic. My biggest challenge seems to be an inability to make arms, so I just don't bother. I like to pretend this is a style choice, when it's really just incompetence.

Ironically enough, this late-onset domesticity was brought about by my discovery of Etsy in the summer of 2006. It had an immediate effect on my pleasure center, like a sort of homemade heroin, and I was instantly hooked. I sat at my computer for hours, looking at page after page of beautifully crafted things and depleting my PayPal account, suddenly oblivious to the fact that I would never wear a skirt with an owl on it.

It would have been dangerous enough if just the shopping region of my brain had been stimulated. But it was the crafting button that really got pushed. I had seen what people could do with a needle and thread, and I wanted to join the party, even though I wasn't invited.

Still, I knew my limitations. That's the most important thing, I think: to know when you reach your stained-glass ceiling.

There was no way, for example, I'd ever be able to knit. That requires needles and math, a terrible combination for someone like me. And I quickly ruled out crochet hooks, candle wax, and anything with knives, glass, or fire.

So it all seemed ordained when my friend Gina told me she had a brand-new beginner-level sewing machine, still in the box, sitting in storage. Clearly the universe wanted me to sew. And who am I to argue with destiny?

Now, in my defense, I should make it clear that I do have some sewing experience. I made a gym bag in junior high, for example, and a brown dress using a pattern and one of those wheel things and chalk. So I've put in my time. Of course, the dress never fit properly, but that's only because both of my arms are the same size.

They say the definition of insanity is doing the same thing over and over and expecting different results, but I didn't think that applied here. After all, I was older now, and tended to read directions more thoroughly than when I was a teenager. And I like to think I have a good deal more patience now. Of course, I also like to think that peanut M&M's don't make you fat because they're magic.

The sewing machine arrived, and I began making toys. After a few disturbing failures that not even the dogs would play with, I did what any poor craftsman does: I blamed my tools. Clearly I needed more things. Things I didn't have. Things I couldn't name but knew I was missing. So I hotfooted it down to the craft store, which, as luck would have it, was only a few blocks away.

This is when the shopping really started. Pins, needles, thread, felt, yarn, pinking shears—everything I needed to affect the demeanor of someone who knew what they were doing. And it was about to get even better. Because now I had to buy things to put these things in!

As much as paraphernalia delights me, nothing gets me giddier than having a tidy little place to store it. Things specifically created to house certain objects are like a drug to me, and sewing is lousy with them.

Thread spool holders, needle separators, bead boxes . . . containers that serve no other purpose than to hold those things and those things only. And if you can find a container that's shaped like the thing that goes in it—like, say, a scissors container shaped like a pair of scissors—well, that's it. I'm spent just thinking about it.

And so, $150 later, I was back home with bags of things that had to be put into other things, an activity that delighted me more than actual crafting.

And even with everything in its place, with fabric to work with and endless possibilities before me, I found myself making some of the shittiest toys imaginable. Misshapen, asymmetrical, accidentally sewn backward so the hair was inside the doll when I was finished, and generally just so pathetic that a child would rather read than play with one.

Yes, I may have gotten a dining room table full of crap at the craft store, but I didn't come home with talent. And I finally realized that all the sundries in the world wouldn't fill that void.

No, for that you need a really expensive sewing machine.

Numb Nuts

Vasectomy Vern doll

$30.00

Description

Vern is approx 7 inches tall and comes with his very own felt bag of frozen peas that can be held in his hand or gingerly placed elsewhere.

There's nothing a man wants more after getting his scrotum cut open than to sit on the couch with a fucking felt doll. Good times.

RockBot

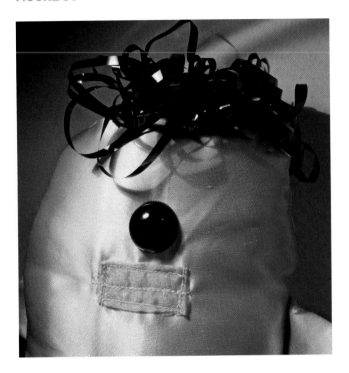

$18.75

Description

RockBot loves music! He is stylin' in gold satin, ready for the dance floor.

RockBot's hair is recycled too – from a cassette tape of Sting's Dream of the Blue Turtles.

Normally I'm not all that interested in recycling, but I'll support anything that destroys one of Sting's tapes.

Baby Sucks-a-Lot

Red Hair mouth eye vampire doll

$100.00

Description

vampire girl. her face was smashed and then repositioned teeth where her eyes should be. dirtied and blood stained vintage dress. bloomers and shoes.

Baby Sucks-a-Lot™, the doll that bleeds, feeds, and even talks! With electronic phrases like "Mmm, good!," "Baby sleepy!," and "I am the angel of death. The time of purification is at hand!"

Warning: Do not use in sunlight.

Bertha the Pregnant, Birthing, Nursing Sock Monkey

$105.00

Description

Bertha, the pregnant sock monkey carries her "baby" in her "womb", and the baby can be "delivered" naturally with its "cord" and "placenta". The cord can be "cut" by unsnapping it from the baby's "belly".

Someone is "out" of their fucking "mind".

Dirty Pillows

Grandma Pillow No More So Word Up

$38.00

Description

Grandma couch pillow looking at me too much and I fixING that!! They're watching. This talisman will banish them.

Look at the cute little pillow bear! Here you go, sweetheart, why don't you go play with—OH MY GOD IT HAS TITS

Peter Rotten Tail

Floppy Calico Bunny Rabbit softie

$40.00

Description

This delightful calico floppy bunny is just waiting to be your friend. With his bright eyes and cheeky nose he is just too cute!

If I was a little kid and woke up on Easter to find this in my room,
I would never stop screaming. And I would convert to Judaism.

I Want to Believe

Wikette – Alien Doll Handmade by Kathleen

$20.00

Description

One thing that makes her unique is the fact that a walnut was used for her head.

If you have any questions feel free to contact me.

---

1. What am I looking at?
2. Where did the alien get the horse? Is it an alien horse? If so, does it contain nuts?
3. What if I wanted the head made out of a filbert?
4. How much is shipping to Earth?
5. Can I buy this if I have squirrels?

Not a Creature Was Stirring

Angel of Death Doll

$149.00

Description

12" tall, original doll. Made with Polymer clay, acrylic paint,
a glass bottle, cloth, chain, feathers, and card stock

I'll never forget the Christmas my parents gave me an Angel of
Death doll. I was so excited I took it to school and the principal died.
True story.

Real Housecats of Orange County

Mizzy – the hoity-toity lolita cat

$99.00

Description

she is all handmade with love: made of wool fabric, felt and some recycled materials for her eyes and lolita skirt. the stuffing is 100% polyester fibre. for her eyes I used swarovsky cut beads and pink beads for a sparkling effect.

Am I the only one who thinks this looks like Star Jones?

In the course of working on Regretsy, I've discovered that there are three major themes in crafting:

1. Bodily functions
2. Fairies
3. Vaginas

The first one is fairly self-explanatory. If it comes out of your body, it can be memorialized in paint, clay, yarn, soap, or wax. I've seen urine-sample candles, ear-wax teddy bears, plush sperm, and soap that looks like turds. And those are just the things I haven't blocked out.

The fairy theme is a little more complex, due in part to its mind-boggling popularity. A quick search for "fairies" on Etsy shows more than 43,000 entries, which is even more staggering when you consider that the majority of these products are made for adults.

Fairy craft can be broken down into three subsets, listed in order of ascending irritation:

1. Fairy art: conventional representations of fairies, such as drawings, paintings, and sculpture. The most accessible subset of fairy craft, fairy art is created for the appreciation of the object itself, or for inherent symbolism that I have no interest in understanding.

2. Fairy wear: articles of clothing or accessories created to assist the wearer in looking like, acting like, or becoming an actual fairy. Items in this subset include, but are not limited to, wings, crowns, scepters, pointy

shoes, prosthetic ears, and shredded diaphanous garments, usually in plus sizes.

3. Fairy tracks: miniature objects created as evidence of the existence of fairies. This is, to me, the most annoying subset of fairy craft, as it assumes a shared belief that sprites live among us and will appear when we need help with farmwork. Whether this is an actual belief or hive-minded whimsy is immaterial; I'm still irritated when I come across a listing for tiny sparkling fairy shit in a vial.

All this insanity is followed by the most cloying part of all: ye olde fanciful sales pitch. "I awoke one mourning and found this wee faerie nest in the round barrows nigh Fairy Toot in Somerset!" No, you really didn't. You walked around your apartment complex and took pictures of a wad of lint in a tree. Then you posted it so some other idiot could buy it and pretend *they* found it in a tree, and the cycle continues unabated.

Finally, we come to perhaps the most puzzling theme in crafting: vaginas.

A few days before I started Regretsy, I happened upon a seller who made disturbingly realistic mini-vaginas in polymer clay. These were then affixed to key chains and necklaces, because, well, why wouldn't they be?

Of course, these weren't just any disturbingly realistic mini-vaginas. These mini-bajingos were painstakingly crafted to *look like your very own*. In fact, the seller included this paragraph in the listing:

> After purchasing, send me an email describing your vagina: the shape of your inner and outer labia, colors, how much or how little your inner labia extend out from your outer labia, how well hidden your clitoris is, is it heavily hooded, or can you see it fairly easily.

This really made me uncomfortable. I mean, I'm fine with my vagina; there's no animosity there. I just think describing your vagina in graphic detail to a stranger over the Internet is wrong, especially if you're paying. And anyway, how many people really want their cooter on a key chain?

Well, apparently a lot of people. As of this writing, the artist has sold 740 of them. This was not about one artist with a vagina jones. It turns out that the crafting world is by and large obsessed with all things vaginal. Yes, vulvacraft, as I like to call it, is thriving.

Like fairy crafting, vulvacraft can also be broken down into subsets. There's practical and/or educational vulvacraft, such as tampon cases, fertility trackers, and reusable sanitary products. Then there's artistic vulvacraft, such as ceramic vaginas or paintings ranging from vaginal impressionism to cervical realism. And finally there's a sort of whimsy vulvacraft, like vagina-shaped lollipops, crocheted vagina water-bottle cozies, felt vaginas on trucker hats, and even teddy bears with vaginas sewn into them.

I'll admit, I'm not a fan. One vagina is plenty, as far as I'm concerned. I don't need a ceramic bajingo on my coffee table, and I don't want to hand my own vagina to the valet at a steak house. But I guess one girl's ceiling is another's pelvic floor.

There is one subset of this theme that completely escapes me: feminist vulvacraft. These are objects created for the purpose of making a statement. And they may very well do that—but they aren't doing it in a language I can understand.

Feminist vulvacraft is—you should pardon the expression—in your face: T-shirts with vaginas airbrushed on them, skirts with giant felt labia on the outside, stuffed uterus plush toys, golden vulva necklaces offset with pearls. Not to mix metaphors, but this stuff is, well, nuts.

I'm not suggesting we should dislike our vaginas, or be ashamed of them, but what's with all the high-fiving and backslapping? It's just a vagina. Lots of people have them. Maybe not everyone you think, but that's another issue.

And really, is it that much greater than having a penis? I don't think so. Yes, you can have a baby, but try making one all by yourself. And if you don't want a baby, you've really leveled the playing field. You still have to bleed every month, and you don't even get to pee standing up.

My point, and I do have one, is that having a vagina is not an accomplishment. It may be what makes you biologically female, but what does that have to do with feminism? Women had vaginas before they could vote or own property, and they didn't get those rights by pinning needle-felted vajayjays to their mantelets.

Keep in mind that if women start defining ourselves by our genitalia, men will do the same. Which means that on any given day, you could be in line at the bank behind a guy wearing a giant crocheted dick on a chain. And frankly, I'm not ready for that.

Madame Ovary

Yes they are uterus earrings!

$15.00

Description

Love your uterus? These may be for you!

These uteri are tiny, hot pink, shimmery and dangle from your ears. I specially mix this polymer clay to have a slight shimmer, vibrant color and excellent durability.

Oh, good. Now I can really hear my biological clock ticking.

vagina credit card holder

$99.00

Description

This beautiful textile sculpture is roomy enough to hold up to 10 cards or could be used to hold coins, cash, condoms or jewelry.

Each of my Vaginas are Handmade and One of a Kind.

This is perfect for my Gap gift card.

Cut the Cord

Childbirth Education Doll PATTERN

$14.89

Description

The pattern is for the experienced crocheter and includes all information for making the Mama and baby (with detachable placenta and umbilical cord).

I'm sorry, but this is terrifying. You want to give this to a child? I'm a grown woman, and I want to lock myself in the laundry room. Seriously, when you're following a pattern to crochet a placenta, you need a time-out. Put this whole thing in the trash and go to Toys "R" Us. Your kid is going to grow up to hate you anyway. Don't rush it.

Paging Dr. Freud

Vulva No. 3

$32.00

Description

Third in an ongoing series, this piece is a completely unique pendant in the shape of a vulva with a coffee bean shaped brown glass bead for the clitoris.

Hand-shaped from 14 gauge Argentium sterling silver wire and hammered for texture and strength, the pendant is 2.4" long and 1.25" at the widest point. The wire ends are soldered in place for strength. It is shown strung on a 26" adjustable knotted brown cord.

Whoa. You could crack walnuts with that thing.

The Curse

Sexy Vampire Reusable Menstrual Goddess XL/Postpartum Cloth Pad

$12.00

Description

An extra long version of the Goddess pad, measuring at a whopping 16 inches long it's surely to be the only pad you'll need for your heaviest overnight flows or after childbirth.

I think most women feel pretty hot after childbirth, so it's about time they get something sexy to bleed on for a couple of weeks. And let me tell you, this hunky vampire really gets you tingling down there! Although that could just be the episiotomy.

Placenta Piece

Handcrafted Placenta

$17.00

Description

lumiknits handcrafted placentas are made from precut felt, which then has detail needlefelted on and a needlefelted umbilical cord attached. They are then stuffed and handsewn together for that uniquely lumpy placenta look.

What exactly do you do with a handcrafted placenta? Do you leave it out on the coffee table? Do you put it in a shadow box? Do you spray Endust on it and run it over the piano? I mean, you can't even really play with it. At least put some googly eyes on it. Then you can put it in a tree on Halloween.

Grandma's Pie

Old Lady Vagina Panties – Size S/M

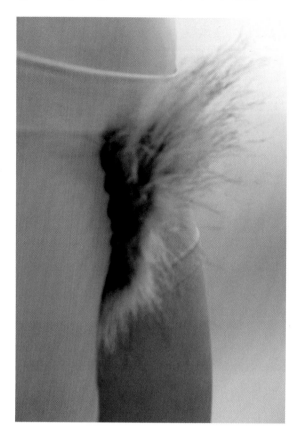

$15.95

Description

These hair panties have grey faux fur that will not shed. These panties were originally designed for my New Orleans based dance troupe called the Bearded Oysters. These are surprisingly versatile.

Well, you can't go wrong with a product called Old Lady Vagina.

Unfortunately, I already have one.

Plug Rugs Woollen Key Chain Tampon Cozies

$4.00

Description

Hand crocheted from unused thrift store wool

"Unused thrift store wool" sounds like the least sanitary thing in the world to store a tampon in, short of a used coffee filter. Not to mention the fact that it attaches to your keys and sits in the bottom of your purse all day, which greatly increases the possibility of getting a piece of Dentyne in your uterus.

Womb with a View

Fetus maternity shirt

$25.00

Description

Poly maternity shirt. A window to the beautiful baby that's inside your womb. With legs conveniently positioned to be either a girl or boy, this baby is calmly sucking on its thumb, and is now on display for all to see.

Great for expectant moms, or effeminate men who've let themselves go!

Red Vadge of Courage

Diving feminine yonni necklace

$20.00

Description

This very special necklace combines the elegant curves of a yoni, or vulva with the simple organic spiral hemp necklace. The pendant is only reminiscent of a yoni-form, not anatomically correct.

FOR GOD'S SAKE, NO ONE WANTS TO SEE YOUR CLAYBIA!

Menstrual Show

Bedazzled tampon

$35.00

Description

The bedazzled tampon you receive will look nearly identical to the bedazzled menses buddy that you see before your very eyes.

If your dad wants to know what it is . . . it's a sparkly candle.

If your dad doesn't know what this is, he's never seen vagina. So unless he's gay, you're adopted.

Light Days, Heavy Nights

Menstrual night

$23.00

Description

"Menstrual Night" – A print of the original painting by Emily Balivet; Acrylic on canvas, 2006.

Left to right: Alice, Vera, and Flo.

When I was about five years old, my father got a TV deal in Hollywood. I don't remember the trip, but I'm told my parents packed us all up and we drove from New York to California, stopping only at Howard Johnsons along the way. My mother reasoned that seeing the same turquoise and orange décor at every meal would be reassuring for the children, and she may have been right. I still find the color combination very soothing.

When we got to California, we moved into a big house in the San Fernando Valley with orange trees and a pool, and my mother immediately started decorating it. She had always been a creative person, but there was something about coming to Los Angeles that turned her into the Evel Knievel of décor. No risk was too great.

The screened-in back patio developed a raging case of Polynesia and magically became the "lanai." Our aesthetic suddenly went from Whitestone to Waikiki, despite the fact that my mother hated the beach. Fishing nets appeared on the walls, laden with blue and green glass floats, and grass mats lined the floor. Wicker, heretofore unknown, was plentiful on Patio Island, and imposing carvings sprang up almost overnight, glowering at anyone who would dare to use the laundry room. My mother also began playing a lot of Harry Belafonte records around this time, for reasons that are still unclear.

But the lanai couldn't hold a tiki torch to the rest of the house, which was slowly being done over in my mother's favorite palette. And when I say "palette," I mean aqua. There was high-gloss aqua paint on almost every surface in that house, making it ideal for mermaids or anyone with macular degeneration.

Nowhere was this more apparent than the kitchen, which had the added glamour of matching appliances. I don't know where she found an aqua refrigerator and stove, but God love her, she had a vision of love, just like Mariah Carey. And we would sit there in that hideous kitchen every night, trying to block it out.

The aqua menace spread to the backyard, where the previous owners had built a sort of concrete "moat" around the perimeter. Lined with rocks and powered by a pool pump, the moat was meant to suggest that our house just happened to be in the path of a natural babbling brook. Of course, living three blocks from the freeway made that somewhat unconvincing, so my mother suggested that my father paint over the gray concrete to add realism. Maybe with a blue of some kind. You know, the color of water.

He didn't even have to go to the hardware store. We had aqua paint stocked up like some families have paper towels.

Painting the moat took days, and my father started getting loopy. After he'd painted so many rooms aqua and had now spent the better part of a week stooped over, painting a concrete runnel, his depth perception went out the window and he painted right over his work boots. He didn't even notice it until he tried to come into the kitchen. My mother laughed so hard she nearly peed her pants, and my dad continued to wear his blue boots to the hardware store every weekend.

When we moved to our next house, it was the seventies. Mom's aesthetic had changed again, but it hadn't mellowed. Now it was all about zebra skin rugs, fur pillows, and tribal carvings. The living room wallpaper was a jungle scene in earth tones. The furniture was reupholstered in giraffe print and burnt-orange velour. There was an enormous yak rug under a glass-topped wrought iron table, and an open staircase led up to a writer's loft. It looked like big-game hunters had come in and redone the *Brady Bunch* set.

What my mother lacked in practicality, she made up for in discomfort. You could either sit in rickety *African Queen* chairs, or on three-legged wooden stools with braided leather seats. Those supposedly came from a monastery, and I can only assume they were used as a form of penance.

Not being comfortable was a sort of leitmotif in her decorating. The TV was always in a room with no couch, and in this house, she chose the kitchen. You had to sit at the table to watch cartoons, and the chairs were space-age egg shapes that were barely tolerable for the time it took to eat your cereal. Even our dishes were hard to use. We had mix-and-match enamelware in plum and olive green, which made a horrible squeaking noise whenever it came into contact with silverware. I recall spending many dinners balancing in the egg chairs, trying to pick food up off the plate without allowing the fork to go all the way through whatever I was eating. It's a wonder I didn't become a surgeon.

But perhaps the most memorable thing about that house was that it marked my own first foray into décor. Because it was while we were living there that my mother decided I was old enough to decorate my own room.

I didn't have much input on the rug, because it was just a given that every room in the house would have three-toned shag carpet that was long enough to style with a hairbrush. I did get to choose the colors, though: three shades of brown, which my mother called "Root Beer" (in hindsight, my mother may have been exploiting my love of soda).

The rest of the process was pretty independent, and I recall learning a lot about contrasting and complementary colors, and why giving one or two special possessions lots of space makes them seem even more important. My mother and I visited furniture stores and looked through books, and it was a bit of a turning point for me. You don't have a lot of control over your life when you're a kid, so controlling your environment makes you feel pretty capable. That's a lesson that still serves me well; managing my environment in times of stress makes me feel like I have a handle on things.

I chose a green and white dresser, an apple-green lacquered desk, and a four-poster bed with a white canopy. I also chose plaid wallpaper for one half of the room, and for the other half I went with cartoon monkeys. I had a shelf over my bed where I carefully lined up all my books and records. I selected a toy box that my father and I distressed with chains to look like an old treasure chest, and all my dolls went inside.

Except for the carpet, every single element of the room was my design and my thinking. It wasn't just a kid's room, it was my personality, expressed in a new and exciting way. It was the perfect space for me, and it was all mine.

Then my parents got divorced and we had to move.

Half Past Crap

TIME to Grate

$28.00

Description

This is an old grater I found at my thrift shop. It is covered with rust, scratches, dents, the handle is falling off, etc. I got off most of the old cheese. I did some grate surgery, and attached a clock mechanism and hands.

She got off *most* of the old cheese, so that's good. It only smells a little like a bum's nutsack. Oh, sure, it's not perfect, but *you* try cleaning a cheese grater with a cigarette.

Urine Luck

Peeing Planter

$25.00

Description

This guy is a different kind of planter. He has two feet and his own little cup for when he gets watered too much and has to go!! A small hole between his legs empties into the cup below.

This is a great place to plant your leeks.

Repeat After Me

Whale Flag

$20.00

Description

Wave your flag! Flags are important symbols affirming who we are, showing others what we stand for.

"I pledge allegiance to the flag of the whale, spider web, American Indian blanket, polka dot, basket weave designs, beige fabric, and horses running in the snow of America, and to the republic for which it stands, one nation under God, indivisible, with liberty and justice for all whales, spider webs, American Indian blankets, polka dots, basket weave designs, beige fabrics, and horses running in the snow."

PLAY BALL!

Perfect for Your Home, Van, or Crawl Space!

Pick two serial killers!

$15.00

Description

this set features two serial killers of your choice, so please leave a note when completing your purchase that specifies which two you would like. the pillowcases in this set are both gold with a white/yellow floral border along the sides. each one measures 35" across and 21" from top to bottom.

Oh, don't make me pick. I love them all!

Siegfried and Schadenfreude

Large Mounted Bearded White Tiger Head with Swarovski Crystal Encrusted Features

$189.89

Description

Mounted faux white tiger head.

Eyes and nose have been hand-encrusted with 150 white and pink Swarovski crystals.

The last thing Roy Horn saw at the Mirage.

Hold Me Closer, Tiny Actor

Madonna of the Candelabra

$50.00

Description

This clock features the image of Michael Jackson tenderly holding the Christ Child, Emmanuel Lewis, on his lap. This clock will add solemnity and uniqueness to any room of your home

Feel free to contact me with any questions.

Yeah, I have some questions: What are the flames behind him? Are those angry villagers or the gates of hell? Is that Larry King in the lower right? Where's Blanket? Where's Michael's other hand? And what would Emmanuel Lewis do?

Kthanxbai

Unidentified Fugly Object

Unknown Sea Creature

$25.00

Description

Is it the deadly Madrona Monster of the Georgia Strait? The friendly 5 headed Ballingal fish or just a pretty piece of coral?

You decide!

Jesus, do I have to do everything around here? All right, I'll tell you what. I'll send you $25 and *you* can throw it out.

Chew It Yourself

Gum art painting

$15.00

Description

Gum art is an image created with the medium of chewed gum, each piece of gum is chewed thoroughly to remove the sugars as well as any flavor/scent. The gum is then spread into an image and allowed to sit for at least a week of cure time to stiffen. It is durable, however do not allow your gum art to sit in direct sunlight. This gum art 'painting' is sure to brighten up any room. I can't stop smiling whenever I see it!

Maybe you just have lockjaw.

Innuendo, Out the Other

Beaver log treasure box

$59.95

Description

Here is a lined Treasure box that I made from a log that came from a beaver dam. One end of the box has the original tooth marks from when the beaver cut down the tree. The box has a lined drawer and a hidden secret drawer that has a magnetic latch so it won't open until you want it to.

I already have a beaver treasure box! Of course, I don't use it as much as I used to.

Wine and Cheese

4 Twilight Inspired Halloween Vampire Wine Glasses

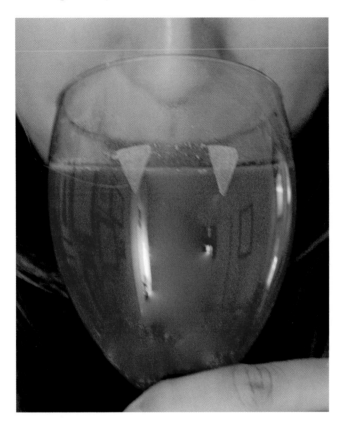

$20.00

Look, I'm a vampire! What? Wait, let me lower the glass a little bit. Okay, now look! What? Okay, how about now? No? Try putting your head on the table and looking up at me. See? It's like I'm drinking blood. Because I have fangs. No, on the glass. No, those are etched in the glass so it looks like I . . . Oh, fuck it.

One of the most common misconceptions about art is that there are no right or wrong answers. Art, they say, is entirely subjective.

It's a charming idea. But anyone who's ever been to art school can tell you that the most brutal, soul-crushing criticism on earth happens in those classrooms. My best friend, now a grown man with a long, successful career as an art director, still blanches at the memory of one of his classes at Art Center. The teacher, a legendary creative director in advertising, would express his displeasure with an illustration by taking out his lighter and actually burning it off the wall. It was an awesome lesson: I don't like it, fuck you.

Still, it's hard to reconcile that kind of criticism with the idea that everything is beautiful in its own way. If art is subjective, then how can anyone tell you that what you're doing is wrong? In fact, how can anyone teach you anything? When everything is right, there's nothing to learn, and no way to improve.

Ultimately, all of this philosophizing leads us to one pretty obvious question: If everything ever created is as good as anything else, why is there so much shit out there?

Well, here's one theory: Maybe it's because the "Beauty is in the eye of the beholder" horseshit is most aggressively advanced by people with no discernable talent. They can pump out the lamest, most misguided crap imaginable, and if you don't like it, it's your fault. "Oh well," they'll say, *"you didn't understand it."* It's genius.

The truth is, there *are* considerations in art—perspective, composition, color, subject matter—elements that make things more visually appealing and draw the viewer in. Technique *can* be learned, and you *can*, in fact, get it wrong.

But even that isn't enough to go by. Because unlike other areas of endeavor, good technique does not guarantee success, and a lack of technical proficiency does not ensure failure. Many brilliant works exist outside of the narrow band of conventionally "good" art. All the color theory and composition classes in the world won't give you talent, and all the talent in the world won't give you soul.

And anyway, who fucking cares? None of it even matters, because your connection to a piece is based on something completely intangible and personal. You might love the picture of a monkey that someone painted with their ass, while the well-composed and academic landscape bores you to tears. Theoretically, anything you feel is right, because art is designed to make you *feel*. Just having a strong response means the artist succeeded.

Theoretically.

Of course, while you might not care why you respond to something, the artists often do. Many prefer that you appreciate the work for the reasons they want you to. If you like a painting because it matches your living room, for example, you're an idiot.

And this is where we often get into trouble on Regretsy, because a lot of the work I feature sells for reasons that the artist may not have intended. Personally, I buy a lot of things that are imperfect or strange, because it amuses me. But that's different from buying something because I think it's good. So the eager patrons on Regretsy find themselves in the strange position of actually offending someone by buying their work.

Of all of the circular, intellectual, clusterfuckery art bullshit, this is the part I have the most trouble with. I can create anything I want, because art is subjective. But your reaction has to jibe with my vision, because *I'm right*. That's like a chef coming out after your dinner and hassling you about why you liked the salad. Who cares? You ate it, you liked it, you paid your tab, and you're coming back. That's a success.

I have a gallery on Regretsy filled with pictures of readers and the pieces they've purchased or received as gifts. I've even received videos of people opening Regretsy presents, and the reactions are all the same: sheer, unmitigated delight.

These are happy people, thrilled to be posing with these crazy pieces that have now become famous in their own way. You can see how proud they are, how connected they feel to their fellow readers, and how much they enjoy being part of a movement.

So I say, let it go. Appreciation is hard to get in this life, and there's no reason to attach so many conditions to it that you can't enjoy it when it finally comes along. A good artist will let his work out into the world and allow people to use it as he or she sees fit.

Of course, that doesn't mean you can use this book as a coaster. I mean, we have to draw the line somewhere.

Snacks on a Plane

Corndog on a Plane

$85.00

Description

Reminds me of the time I flew to New York and had a corndog.
27" x 22" Framed.

Reminds me of the time I saw an $85 painting of a corndog and didn't buy it.

Bird on a Wire

Large hanging raven sculpture

$75.00

Description

This is a (not so) Common Raven, handcrafted in stoneware clay and uniquely textured low fire glaze.

Measuring about 3 feet from wing tip to wing tip, he weighs about 15 pounds, and would make an excellent addition to a room needing a little extra interest.

This is going right over the baby's crib.

It's Always Fun Until Someone Gets Hurt

Digging up bones

$15.00

Description

This is a fun little painting brought on by a story of an abused woman I recently heard. This is a comical take on handling many problems.

There's nothing quite as comical as an abused woman in a graveyard with a shovel. Seriously, it never gets old. If more people solved their problems by abusing women and exhuming corpses, this old world would be a lot more fun.

Rudolph the Roadkill Reindeer

Roadkill Painting

$750.00

Description

"Roadkill 6" 2001 by Raven

This huge oil and acrylic painting was inspired by some photographs I took of a deer hit by a truck in 2001. This painting is the 6th roadkill painting in the series and is signed and dated.

I'm collecting all six roadkill pals! All I need now are Pancake Possum and Stiffy the Squirrel!

I Had a Dream

Princess Demon of hair

$20.00

Description

This is a 9 x 11 inch painting of a dream. I think it morphed from a short story I was working on and got more interesting in my dream. The dream was of a island that was filled with real and completly unreal beings such as the animated pirate teddy bear seen in the picture. In any case the Princess demon of hair was floating, running and just showing up all over the island trying to cut off and some times cut up people for their hair. The teddy bear was trying to escape but had issues with the water. This is the spot where I woke up. She had claimed another victim and the bear had been injured. This may be reproduced in a set of 10 prints.

I had a dream that someone put this painting in a trash can and set it on fire. Oh yeah, your short stories were in there, too.

Melted egg record

$25.00

Description

Here in the middle of the Mojave Desert, it can get really hot. "How hot?" you ask. Hot enough to fry a record on the sidewalk! (((rimshot)))

Artwork is water-resistant and may be wiped occasionally with a damp cloth to keep it dust-free.

This looks really heavy. How much is the shipping?

Attention Horse

A Portrait of a Horse as a Young Man 24x18x1 original

$130.00

Description

A portrait of a horse as a young man openly expressing himself. 24"x18"x1" acrylic on canvas. Ready to Hang.

Is that the title or a list of ingredients?

Robot Tennis Love

$45.00

Description

The robot is playing doubles with a charming companion. you can see the delight in their faces as they play a romantic match together.

Hey, you two, get a Roomba!

Clothes to You

Wedding Dress Painting

$25.00

Description

After my own wedding and realizing that the most expensive piece of clothing I have ever owned was sitting in the closet I decided to create a painting of it.

If you would like your wedding attire turned into a painting you just need to, after purchase, send me a picture.

In about a week I shall create a gorgeous painting. I welcome all dresses and groom attire from the traditional to the indie or goth.

I now pronounce you dress and suit. You may now press your pants.

Flies F*cking

$450.00

Description

"F#%king Flies" by Kelly Hutchison (aka "Dark Vomit").

Original oil painting. Measures 15 inches by 18 inches wide with the gold frame (frame comes with purchase) Professionaly framed. Signed and dated by artist.

"Yeah, just like that. Move your leg. No, your other leg. No, your other leg. No, your other leg. Oh, yeah."

Hoof and Mouth

Brush Up

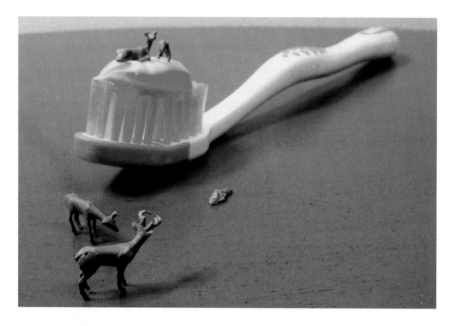

$12.00

Description

Looks great in a bathroom, and it reminds you to brush your teeth!

Approved by the ADA and the NRA.

When you sell your work on Etsy, you first have to choose the category you want to list it in.

It should be relatively easy to do. There are many categories, and many subcategories, so you can list your wares with pinpoint accuracy. Why sell your crocheted Kleenex box cover in Housewares, when you can list it in Houswares > Cozy > Tissue Box Cozy?

But even with such a thorough hierarchy of headings, subheadings, sub-subheadings, and nesting subheading subheads, Etsy still can't keep up with the more adventurous handcrafters, who can make shit faster than they can find a place for it.

To serve as a sort of cyber junk drawer for the unexplainable, there's a category sitting quietly between Dolls and Furniture that goes by the name of *Everything Else*. Or, as I like to call it, *WTF: Level One*.

Once inside the dripping walls of Everything Else, you have a whole host of terrifying subcategories to investigate. And each one leads to something more inexplicable than the one before.

WTF: Level Two
Home > Buy > Categories > Everything Else > Taxidermy

When I first discovered that there were dead things on Etsy, I was pretty stunned. Oh, not "stunned" like some of these animals may have been before getting a wire frame up their ass, but pretty close. And these animals are more than just stuffed; they're decorated. Sure, you can get yourself a nice valu-pak of assorted pigeon feet for all your pigeon-foot crafting needs, but only on Etsy can you find a stuffed feral goat made up to look like a unicorn.

It's a rotating circus of delights in the Taxidermy category, and you just never know what's going to be stuffed and nailed to a board. At the moment, I'm looking at a real bobcat skull painted like one of the guys from Kiss, a handmade hornet's nest (I guess even insects buy handmade), and my favorite so far: a lucky key chain made from a human foot bone. I'm not sure who that's supposed to be lucky for, but I'm going to guess the original owner isn't running after any leprechauns.

And just when you think you've died and gone to Etsy, you see this disclaimer, on a listing for a doll dressed as the grim reaper with a skunk skull for a head:

IMPORTANT NOTE: HUMAN REMAINS CANNOT BE SOLD TO ANYONE IN GEORGIA OR TENNESSEE, WHERE THE POSESSION OR USE OF HUMAN REMAINS IN ART IS PROHIBITED.

Sucks to be you, Georgia and Tennessee!

WTF: Level Three
Home > Buy > Categories > Everything Else > Pocket
This category of Everything Else seems to only demand that you be able to put it in your pocket. Technically speaking, this could be Chapstick, so I don't know how they keep the quality control going.

Fortunately, quality is not an issue. I'm currently looking at a wolf hair amulet for "protection," a very small plush rabbit with the word BITCH embroidered on it, and a "Haunted Ouija board Las Vegas Casino style black jack roulette poker chip," which would probably sell faster if it had more words in the title.

WTF: Level Four
Home > Buy > Categories > Everything Else > Metaphysical
This is where buying handmade really makes a difference. Who among us isn't sick to death of fortune-telling supplies from those big-box stores? I want a hand-carved wand, not some polystyrene McMagic bullshit. And if I see one more Coach or Juicy enchanted pouch for holding my runes, I will cast a spell on your ass.

Fortunately, all your handcrafted "magick" needs are met right here, from tarot cards and ritual kits to homemade potions from chicken-blood-soaked kitchens across the country. Yes, it's all on Level Four, along with a $2,500 spirit portal made of glass beads and wire, ready to transport you to another dimension, where selling fake portals is not prohibited by law.

WTF: Level Five
Home > Buy > Categories > Everything Else > Weird
Well now you're talking! Level Five; home of the ultimate Everything Else fuckery! Forget all those run-of-the-mill wolf hair amulets and human foot bone key chains—that was nothing. That was, like, bridge-and-tunnel weird. That wasn't even—well, but the foot, though, that was pretty fucking weird.

But now we're really rocking the crazy shit. One hundred pages of felt beards, root-beer-can pigs, and a box of fake tapeworms made from spray-painted fettuccine. You're not going to get this at Bed, Bath & Beyond.

My favorite part of this category is the services that are offered: psychics and trance channelers, sitting in their kitchens, smoking Newports and asking thousand-year-old sprites if you should take that job at Kinkos.

And keep your eye out for great bargains. In this economy, everyone is making deals! I've got my eye on a vial of raccoon blood that's going for 30 percent off. I WILL MAKE YOU LOVE ME!

Yes, it's all pretty peculiar in this little corner of the world.

Of course, the really weird part is that most of the items in this chapter came from Housewares.

A Kernel of Truth

Corn Poo Soap

$5.00

Description

Here's another growler! This summer, after a BBQ, you will be looking in the toilet just to see how close this one looks to the real thing!

Get up, turn around, look in the toilet, and compare your turd to the product they just sold you. If only everyone had that kind of honesty.

Fish in a Squirrel Suit Taxidermy

$350.00

I rest my case.

Yeah, We've Got That

MONEY CLIP – 24kt Gold Plated Money Clip –
Great for Fathers Day

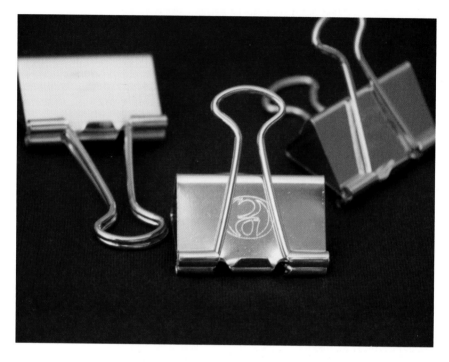

$9.99

It's no secret that dads love office supplies. So this year, why not give him a binder clip? He'll love the way it looks like something on the floor under his desk.

OBAMA TOILET SEAT AND TANK LID COVER SEAT

$23.00

Let the president of the United States inspire you as you push for the passage of last night's burrito.

Curiously Repulsive

Baby Rat in Altoid Tin – Original Mixed Media Sculpture

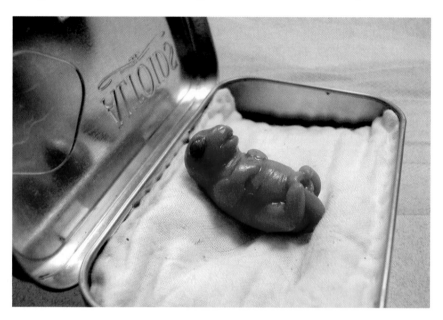

$45.00

The seller of this piece describes it as "really fun," and I have to agree. I don't think there's anything more fun than a baby rat in your mints, unless it's a dead cat in your chimney or maggots in your sink. Oh, man, I'm smiling just thinking about it.

Something Blue

wedding soap – choking hazard

$3.00

Description

***Please use caution when having kids handle this soap, there is a choking hazard.**

You may now perform the Heimlich maneuver.

Ham Sanitizer

Bacon Soap

$3.00

Description

Yes, Bacon Soap.

There is a whole group of people out there who are obsessed with everything bacon!!! When I found this great smoky Bacon scent, I knew I had to make some.

New Bacon for Her™. Because every woman wants to smell like she works at IHOP.

Stiff Upper Lip

Phallic Chapstick Cozy / Lipstick Case / Finger puppet

$6.00

Description

Hand-crocheted in one piece from vegan-friendly cotton yarn, and available in a range of colors. The "head" and "balls" are stuffed with cotton batt, there is a loop for handy attaching to a keyring or purse, and the end is open to firmly encase your chapstick or lipstick, or whatever else you might want to store in there.

"The new Chapstick Cock Cozy: Grab soft lips by the balls!"

I should never have gotten out of advertising.

Lady Caca

Embroidered Toilet Paper MY POKER FACE

$4.00

Description

Embroidered Toilet Paper:
Only the first sheet is embroidered, this can be taken off and saved in a
scrapbook/memory book.
Charmin toilet paper is used. If you prefer a different brand please convo me.

Are there really people who save toilet paper in scrapbooks? Is this
really a thing? And if so, do you call it "crapbooking"?

CONVO ME IF YOU PREFER QUILTED NORTHERN

Green Frogs and Ham

Aardvark's FROG on a SUCCULENT HAM

$42.00

Description

Here's something you need! For the holidays or whenever. This bead measures 38mm long x 31mm high x 23mm wide. Vertical 3/32" bead hole.

I had this for breakfast once in Louisiana.

Bird's-eye View

Doll heads in a bowl of Brussels sprouts

$50.00

Description

Full bleed professional 12x18 print on archival paper, signed on the back with a lustre finish.

Other sizes may be available upon request.

I remember when I was a kid, my mom did everything to get me to eat my doll heads. She even put cheese on them! But it didn't work. I could still see the hair.

Gnome Depot

Miniature Fairy or Dollhouse Toilet with Frog

$33.00

Oh, good. Somebody finally managed to combine two of the biggest obsessions in crafting: mythical creatures and bodily functions. Now, if they would just make mermaid tampons, we could all go home.

Christmas is the Kobayashi Maru of holidays. It is unwinnable. Like a wedding or a funeral, Christmas is so full of expectation, we never quite feel like we got it right. No matter what we do, there's always that nagging feeling that we didn't do enough.

It doesn't help that we measure our experiences against a Christmas no one is having, an ideal holiday fantasy created by advertisers trying to sell us shit. All season long, we see images of truly happy people enjoying their families and feeling Christmas spirit, and we're filled with resentment.

We're not having that feeling, are we? We don't want to leave cookies for Santa or make snow angels in front of the rectory. We want to upend the holiday table and bludgeon our sister-in-law with a turkey leg, because frankly, that bitch has been asking for it all year. And if we don't want to do that, well, we'd at least like to just go home and drink cough syrup.

We're set up to fail. And we don't just fail ourselves during the holidays, we fail the people we love, and we do it every time we go Christmas shopping. Because no matter how much thought and effort we put into finding the perfect gift, it ultimately falls short if *we didn't make it ourselves.*

Oh, sure, that's a beautiful coat you gave your mother. But if you really loved her, you'd have knit it with your own hands. Preferably out of recycled fucking plastic bags, so you could have loved the planet too.

How did this happen? How did handcrafting become the new standard for meaningfulness? I hear a lot about the commercialization of Christmas, but handcrafting is becoming as pretentious and annoying as any trendy brand you feel obligated to buy. Maybe even more so, because it also assumes a certain moral superiority over store-bought gifts.

It's hard to know whether magazines are fueling it or reacting to it, but every December issue at the checkout stand pimps the "magic" of home-made Christmas. And we stare at them, exhausted, feeling guilty for buying frozen piecrust. If we really loved our families, we'd raise our own Christmas geese in the laundry room. We'd decorate our Christmas trees with homemade candy canes, using recipes handed down from the Nords. We'd boil sugar in copper pots while wide-eyed children waited in sweaters made using yarn we carded ourselves from free-range, bottle-fed alpacas. And Father would wrap hand-carved wooden toys in Mother's embroidered linens and tie the packages up with locks of Grandma's hair, because we love our families too much to buy curling ribbon.

Frankly, I think the whole thing is bullshit, not to mention being terribly unfair. And not just to those who can never achieve the beautiful creations that Martha pretends to make, but to people like me, who are on the receiving end of gifts from people who can't cook or sew to save their lives. The constant message that a handmade Christmas is a *better* Christmas goads even the least talented crafter into turning out some corn-studded yule logs, and that doesn't serve anyone.

I have a friend. She means well. Every year, she makes the most horrific holiday cookies to ever get scraped off a baking sheet. I refer to them as "window clings," because they're thin and sticky, and perfect for using as car decals. I'm not sure what she's doing wrong, but she appears to be leaving out whatever ingredient is necessary to make them cookies, instead of, say, silicone pot holders.

And this happens every year, because no one will tell her the truth. No one will say, "You know how everyone says handmade things make Christmas more special? Well, my Christmas would be more special if you bought me something from Costco."

Why don't we do that? Why don't we just tell people that they don't have to feel compelled to make things, and in fact, maybe they shouldn't? Maybe they should just buy us some small, thoughtful token, because perhaps they're better at choosing something than creating it, and ultimately, that would make us happier?

Well, because that would be *mean*. It's much kinder to allow her to bake year after year and pretend we like her cooking, even though we're just going to throw it in the trash as soon as she leaves. Then we can all make fun of her behind her back. Yes, that's the decent thing to do.

And you know, when you come right down to it, that's really what Re-gretsy is. It's you and me, laughing at the horrible sweater your aunt makes you every year for Christmas because you don't know how to ask her not to. Except it's not your aunt. And there's no sweater. And also this is a book, which she could be reading.

The point is, we used to worry that we didn't *spend* enough, and now we worry that we didn't *make* enough. Maybe we can learn to split the difference.

For example, maybe this year I can just get one dozen cookies from my friend and, say, a Barnes & Noble gift card. Which I can use to buy her a cookbook.

Win-win.

Goys for Tots

Holiday Stocking

$6.00

Description

Now there is a holiday stocking for almost all of us! Here is our orthodox holiday stocking with payot made of brown and black pipe cleaners.

Crisper than matzoh, his schleppers they came,

And he kvetched, and he nudged, and call'd them by name:

"Oy, Dasher! Oy, Dancer! Oy, Moishe and Aaron!

"Oy, Herschel! Oy, Moses! Oy, Yitzchak and Yaron!"

And I heard him exclaim as he headed for home,

"You should live and be well, and I bid you shalom!"

Jesus Christ, That's a Big Bird

Dove and Baby Jesus Ornament

$17.00

Description

A blue ribbon ties around bird neck for those blistery winter nights and has a loop to hang on your holiday tree. Baby has gold halo attached.

I don't remember the part of the story where the giant bird swooped in and took the baby Jesus back to her nest and fed him to her chicks. But then, I am half Jewish.

Meerkat Manger

Christmas Nativity Meerkats

$55.00

Mongoose 2:15–20

When the angels had left them and gone into heaven, the shepherds said to one another, "Let's go to Bethlehem and see the meerkats, which the Lord has told us about on Animal Planet." So they hurried off and found Mary and Joseph and the baby, who were living in a large underground network with multiple entrances. When they saw the child, they scent-marked the subordinates of the group to express their authority, and this was followed by much grooming and licking of faces.

Conjoin Us for the Holidays

Tiny Twins Embryo Ornament

$7.25

Description

This tiny twin sprout is only 1" long (not including the loop on top).

Comes with a red ribbon.

Boy, this takes me back! When I was a kid, my sisters and I would always fight over who got to hang the Siamese polyspermic zygote on the tree.

Jesus Is the Reason for the Season Tickets

Jesus was a Yankee fan

$150.00

Description

An antique beaten copper image of Mary and the baby Jesus inspired me to paint it as such. It measures 12" x 9" and is maybe 1/8" to 1/4" thick in some parts. a great gift for any sports fan!

For God so loved the world, He gave up a bases-loaded walk.

epilogue

Whenever I press Publish on a post, it's a crapshoot.

For the most part, people have no idea that they're going to be featured on Regretsy. I don't have to ask permission to criticize work that's posted on Etsy, and I usually don't. It's like the Wheel of Shit, and you never know when it's going to land on you.

Obviously, people can only react in two ways: they either like it or they don't. I'm happy to say that the people who like being featured far outweigh the people who don't (in fact, I can count on one hand the number of sellers who have asked that their pieces be taken down). Generally, sellers are so adept at putting it all in perspective and seeing the humor in it that I feel like Emo McWeepypants in comparison.

The people who impress me the most are the ones who run with it. For example, after I featured a beaded butterfly brooch that readers described as looking "like it was hit by a car," the seller posted new photos, showing the brooch under a tire and stuck to a windshield. The brooch sold immediately, and she has a new legion of fans.

Also rising to the occasion was the seller of the cheese-grater clock, who identified his cigarette-smoking model as yours truly, and suggested we were in a romantic relationship.

Still other sellers, like the maker of the corn-studded poo soap, have joined the site as regular commenters, struck up partnerships with other featured sellers, and created Regretsy-inspired merchandise that has sold out quickly. One woman makes necklaces with miniature replicas of paintings featured on Regretsy, and at last count, she had sold close to one hundred, making them the most popular items in her store.

Ironically, the people who are the most vocal about hating the site have never been featured. Their work is competent and unremarkable, and not really anything I find comedy or wonder in. And maybe that's the whole problem.

Etsy promotes a specific aesthetic on one end of the spectrum, and Regretsy promotes one on the other. But where is all the media attention and noise for the people in the middle? Well, there isn't any, because it's the middle. And the middle is boring as shit.

Nothing is really all that engaging without a strong point of view. And let's face it, having a point of view is a risk, because it immediately creates an opportunity for the opposite perspective. So if I'm just vanilla, you'll love me, right? Well, not if I like chocolate. Taste is not universal, as evidenced by the fact that John Tesh has sold more than five million records.

It must all seem exactly backward to these craft hobbits of Middle Earth, who can't see why their perfectly pleasant work isn't being celebrated. It has to be galling to think you're playing by the rules and getting no rewards while the idiots who make fetus-shaped catnip toys are riding the Regresty wave to *The Wall Street Journal* and selling out their stores.

One of those rules, and easily the most overrated, is being *nice*. There really is an almost pathological need to be supportive when it comes to crafts, no matter how shitty they are. I could feature a vest made of panty liners, and I guarantee you someone would feel compelled to say, "Boy, that sure looks absorbent!"

This kind of obsessive-compulsive complimenting is particularly prevalent on Etsy, where even constructively criticizing another seller brings the cone of silence down and locks the thread. And to be perfectly frank, that's the kind of "We're all winners" mentality that's turning us into pussies and liars.

I know a couple with an eight-year-old daughter. She came home from school one day with the news that she was in a play called *The Seven Snow Whites*. At first they thought she'd made some charming little error, but then they saw the flyer. And by God if the starring role hadn't been given to seven different girls, who would all be onstage at the same time, taking turns speaking the lines. Apparently the school didn't want to send the message that one child might actually be better at something than the others, so they gave everyone a trophy.

I was not raised to believe this kind of bullshit. There was only one Snow White in the movie I saw; that's what made her special. Sure, there were seven dwarves, but even they had different names. Were they all supposed to be doctors?

In my family, winning and losing was not some abstract concept; it was the way my father provided for us. He was an entertainer, and he spent his life competing with other talented men for jobs. He won more jobs than most people, but he lost quite a few as well. You can't do that very long without developing some strategies for coping with rejection.

That doesn't mean it wasn't challenging. I vividly recall one night when I was about seven, watching him brood in front of the television. He had been auditioning for a lot of jobs, but not getting the parts he wanted.

Suddenly he stood up, took off his shoe and hurled it at the television set. "Jesus Christ!" he shouted. "Who do you have to blow to get on *Get Smart?*"

I never forgot that moment, primarily because my mother wouldn't tell me what that meant.

But despite those occasional frustrations, my father went on to have a very long, successful career as an artist. The trick for him was to be unflinching in his vision while still being honest about his shortcomings. And doesn't that seem healthier in the long run, to have balance? Not every bad thing you hear is ignorance and jealousy; not every good thing you hear is the truth. Dismiss all negativity and you'll never learn anything.

People ask me if I think a backlash is coming against the snarky humor that's gotten so popular lately. I tell them that snark *is* the backlash—against the sunshine enemas we're all being forced to administer to anyone with a glue gun. It's frustrating to have to reinforce people who are undeserving of your praise. I realize you may not want to hear that the brown tie-dye you used on your scarf looks like someone wiped their ass with it, but that's what people are thinking. I'm just saying it out loud.

Having a negative judgment is human, and keeping it to yourself is only temporary. No matter how hard you clamp down on it, you will eventually find a loophole that lets the truth come out. I've had people tell me that it's all right not to like something, provided you only tell your spouse. Others say it's okay to laugh at someone's work with your friends, but not strangers. And one woman said it was okay to make fun of someone's work, but not on a website. Even the biggest doe-eyed, pearl-clutching Etsy muffin has to find some way to make it okay to be negative, because we have no choice.

Ironically, many of these niceaholics are crueler than I could ever be. I had a woman tell me she hoped I'd get cancer again, because I made a joke about her hat. Someone reported Regretsy to Facebook as a site that "promotes hate speech." And a few people actually wrote to Random House, begging them to cancel the book and never work with me again. These letters are generally written by the same people who say, "If you don't like my work, just don't look at it." So I guess consistency is only for plaster of Paris.

Personally, I'm not big on shutting people down, because it means that I could lose my right to self-expression. After all, your right to be an asshole virtually guarantees my right to be one, too. I sometimes try to explain this to people who write to me, and I point out that denigrating my work isn't much different from what I do. It usually ends with them telling me I'm stupid or old, or making fun of my hair.

The great irony, of course, is that I'm not the first to judge these people; I'm just the first they noticed. If they were paying attention, they'd see that people have been judging them from the day they opened their stores. What do you think traffic is, anyway? Every view without a sale is another person who didn't like your shit enough to buy it.

Not everything is good, nor should it be. There is a great need for bad in the world. If nothing was ever bad, we'd have no way of recognizing things that are truly exceptional. We wouldn't even be able to improve as artists, because there would be no difference between our first attempts and the work we produced after a lifetime of learning and experience.

A week or two after Regretsy went live, I happened across a blog by a poet named Arthur Chapin, who was writing about art and criticism and Regretsy. He ended his piece with this quote, which I have saved all these months to my desktop. I look at it periodically because it's just so perfectly crafted and beautifully communicates everything I feel:

Sometimes, when people are uproariously laughing at you or staring at you in bewilderment, it's not because they're trying desperately to mask their fear of the painful truth you bring, it's just because you're a fucking idiot and completely unaware of it.

If I had any talent, I'd put that on a sampler.

acknowledgments

You're not the only person who's suffered through this book. Many people go through hell to put a piece of crap like this in your hands, and this is where I thank them for everything they had to put up with.

My heartfelt thanks to:

John, for loving me even when I didn't take a shower, which was often.

Mick, for coming up with a lot of funny shit that I'll get the credit for.

Gina, for the endless hours of work and support.

Jeremy and Larry, for talking me out of doing that stupid thing that time.

Hostropolis, for hosting the site with no problems ever, and not blinking when the traffic exploded.

Meg, for getting me a book deal and never expressing any doubt—at least, not to me.

Jill, my sainted editor at Random House, for telling me terrifying things in a very calm voice.

The hundreds of crafters who have had the guts and humor to enjoy being featured in the book and on the site.

And the millions of people who have allowed me the honor of making them laugh, which is all I have ever wanted to do.

the last word:
the sellers speak

There is a big difference between honest commentary and tearing down someone's craft in an antagonistic or hateful way. I've spent some time looking at the items on Regretsy, and I'd like to say it's all in good fun, but at times I think it goes too far.

> Michael Phipps, Scatterbrain Tees

If you think something is a horrible piece of shit you should be allowed to say it. Some people really do just make shit and they know that they make shit, and you have to respect them for not caring.

> Vashni De Schepper, Bixbie's Curios

No one should feel obligated to be positive about my artwork. Not all of my artwork is positive.

> Dark Vomit (Kelly Hutchison),
> The Vomitorium

If someone enjoys crafting for the hell of it, you'd have to be kind of an asshole to say something negative about their work. But once you put a price tag on your artistic expression, no one's obligated to keep their yap shut.

> Cathy Lybarger, Aardvark Art Glass

People definitely feel compelled to be positive about handcrafts, but that's why Regretsy is so f-ing funny. It says what people are thinking but are too polite to say.

> Sara E. Lynch, Ducks and Chicks
> and Geese Better Scurry

The mere existence of an object will subject it to discussion and judgment, but I believe that nothing is mean if it's funny enough. Especially if it's the truth.

Morgan Fields, Slightly Curious

I think there has to be a happy medium of showing respect while at the same time being able to voice an opinion, even if it isn't a very popular one. In the end, honesty really is the best policy. No one likes a pity vote.

Erin Rahel, frenzy!

We've seen people make some terrible art, with really controversial subject matter, and they think they have special status that places them above judgment. Then they go online and scream about how childish and vulgar Regretsy is, filling threads with their own childish and vulgar posts, and never see the irony. Anytime we feel like wallowing in hurt feelings about people not liking my crafts, we just think about those people, and remind ourselves that we don't want to turn into one of them.

Elaine Gladney and Billie Balizet,
The Worst Shop Ever

I think those who judge something that was created by a crafter sometimes wish they could be an artist. They spend countless hours looking through thousands of shops hoping to find something they would call "ugly," when in reality they just hate themselves.

Tina Summers,
Cowgirl Heaven

The idea of a culture too polite to talk about what they're experiencing is downright terrifying to me.

Emily Balivet,
The Art of Emily Balivet

Having been struck by the merciless hand that is Regretsy, I feel more solidarity with my fellow crafters. We are all damaged doves flying in awkward circles against the wind.

Fizaa Dosani,
BIG FIZZ House of Camp & Kitsch

It's hard to be too serious about making fairy toilets.

Kevin Stevens and Tori Carpenter,
Fairy Furnishings

A lot of the work I create is political or controversial in nature and not necessarily designed to be "liked." What it is designed to do is provoke debate. Often this debate is about the nature of handmade stuff and our general relationships with stuff in general. If this means someone doesn't like the object, that's fine by me. What interests me is if they can tell me why and what reactions they have to it.

Rayna Fahey, Radical Rags

It's "art" while I'm making it. It's merchandise as soon as it's for sale.

Coy Powers,
CR Powers' Oddities,
Marvels & Curiosity Candles

I had never seen Regretsy before. My initial reaction was: "Whatever." I'm just not that into snarkiness.

Sharon Coleman,
cozycoleman and kippahmitzvah

I only feel obligated to like my grandmother's peanut brittle and anything my son puts his hands on, and really that's about it.

Stacey Gordon, staceyrebecca

I couldn't help but wonder why Regretsy had chosen me. After giving the whole thing some very careful thought I asked myself, "Could it possibly be because you're peddling alien dolls using walnuts for their heads?"

Kathleen Paquette, MyCrafts R 4U

I started screaming, "I'm on Regretsy!" My husband ran in to find me laughing, clapping, and jumping up and down. I love humor, especially dark humor, so being featured was like getting a wish for me. I had a steady increase in traffic and sales. Some people saw it as great free publicity for my shop, while others told me how embarrassed they would be if they were me. One friend—who was also featured on Regretsy—stopped speaking to me because I was not offended.

CappySue,
Cappy Sue Creations

I have loved being on Regretsy! I finally found a place where I belong!
Teena Schorr, SoapyHo

When I found out I had been featured on Regretsy, I was stunned. I felt like I had made it as an artist. I still feel that way.
Terri McNamara, thepurlminx

I think that every crafter should experience Regretsy. It builds character. Or at the very least, it can turn you into one.
donna Valentine,
Valentine Fiber Arts

Being featured on Regretsy is like a swine flu shot: painful at first, but beneficial in the long run.
Eric Masters, IMOTIME

It's nice when items sell, but it's not that important to me. If they don't sell, I give them out as gifts, and I think people are genuinely happy to receive them (except for April, who has refused multiple times).
Terri McNamara, thepurlminx

I wish I could say that being featured on Regretsy has led to my being more focused on crafting and promoting my items on Etsy. But the truth of the matter is, my goat is going through her first pregnancy and I'm so focused on her right now I'm not getting much done at all.
Jennifer Grant,
Goose On The Loose Jewelry

I was getting 60–70 hits per hat before the Regretsy listing, now I average about 180 quick hits, then a sale. What's significant is that the YouTube video associated with it went from about 250 hits before Regretsy to over 52,000.
John Henderson,
RoyRoadFishCompany

It's difficult to say if being featured on Regretsy has been positive or negative. I'm fine with it and I can laugh, but I haven't told my parents.

Justine S., JustineJustine

When I saw that I was featured, I braced myself for the comments to come, as I knew there would be those who consider reusable menstrual pads disgusting. Instead I found some very witty comments like "He's into red-hot showers." It got over 13,251 hits and sold the same day.

Hope Walston, Mimi's Dreams

My sales have increased immensely since being featured on Regretsy. I have received a lot of nice feedback from strangers, as well as some hate mail from religious fanatics. I really can't believe how angry some people get over a felt catnip toy. All I can say to them is Jesus loves you, too.

Vashni De Schepper,
Bixbie's Curios

I received an email inquiry from a lady who had seen my work on Regretsy. In my wildest dreams I did not realize there were so many ways of looking at one feathered ring.

Leanne Angwin, StudioLeanne

The best part of being featured was seeing some of my serious crafty friends on Facebook and Twitter linking to Regretsy and commenting on how they'd "just die" if any of their items got featured. I took great delight in pointing out my appearances!

Rayna Fahey, Radical Rags

I don't need people to understand me or the things I make. I just need them to have a PayPal account.

Kym Joseph,
Crafty is the new black

It is less important to be liked or understood than it is to be paid. I am shallow and easily deciphered, but I could always use more admiration and love.

Shing Yin Khor, Specimen7

There isn't much stuff I do that's meant to be understood. And if you claim to understand, quit it.

Brooks Werner, Hautestew

I get the prima donna, uptight, holier-than-thou types emailing me all the time, telling me that my adult soaps are too sexual. I just tell them to go to church and pray for me.

Teena Schorr, SoapyHo

Generally, I don't think it's important that people understand or like your work, because who gives a fuck what other people think? 99.5% of people are assholes.

Vashni De Schepper,
Bixbie's Curios

I get lots of hate mail and it makes me laugh. It isn't important that others understand me. I don't understand myself half the time.

Bastet2329, Creepy Dolls

I still don't understand what would motivate a person to macrame an owl.

Jennifer Grant,
Goose On The Loose Jewelry

Who am I to try to control the way my art is received in the minds of anyone else in the world? That's not my job. My job is to make myself giggle.

Stacey Gordon, staceyrebecca

I'm a taxidermist because I enjoy it. I like making things that I can't or won't buy for myself. And sometimes I get to eat a weird animal that most people probably haven't heard of.

Morgan Fields, Slightly Curious

I got into crafting because I needed something active to do while I watched reruns of *Magnum P.I.*

Kyley Quinn, Latebloomers Art

I started collecting bones and painting roadkill about ten years ago. I grew up in Pennsylvania and there is roadkill everywhere. It is just impossible to ignore the corpses on the side of the road. It just seemed a waste to let the animals rot away, so now I make pretty things from them.

> Raven Young,
> Dreadful Things By Raven

I got into crafting to try to earn my parent's love and respect. It hasn't worked yet.

> Fizaa Dosani,
> BIG FIZZ House of Camp & Kitsch

Obviously I've learned that not everyone wants faux meat on their head, and I don't take that personally.

> Heather M. Hopp,
> Heather's Feathers and Fluff

I'd love to be understood—but hey, this is the Internet, and I'm a weird girl making miniature vulva jewelry. I'm not holding my breath.

> Ashleigh Heather Russell,
> tangerined

It's important to remember that what you do isn't who you are. Once you start selling your work on the Internet, it's open season, so it's imperative that you not take it or yourself too seriously. Otherwise, as my grandmother used to say, "this can only end in tears."

> Michael Quinn, Glampire Design

I am not my crafts. I am, however, my art.

> Cybele, Cybelesque

When you're creating something using your skill, talent, and hard work, it becomes a part of you. But realistically, there's a big difference between me, all the various things that make up who I am, and a crocheted penis that I made in an evening.

> Jennifer Talley, The Naughty Hook

My art is an extension of myself, and criticizing it is the same as criticizing the essence of my being. It is more me than I am.

> Fizaa Dosani,
> BIG FIZZ House of Camp & Kitsch

Art and crafts are just things. I put a lot of my own expression into them, but they aren't me any more than a photograph is.

> Sheryl Westleigh, Noadi's Art

I feel that people have an obligation to be positive about my handcrafts, but everything else is fair game.

> Hannah Pierro, Mistress Hannah

I spent four years in art school having my work judged on a daily basis. It was never a personal attack. I find that the online community tends to have trouble separating the two. I don't take it personally. The German insults are particularly creative.

> Sharon Coleman,
> cozycoleman and kippahmitzvah

In all artistic endeavors, you must be willing to accept criticism. Having the ability to laugh and joke with someone (or punch them in the face and get away with it) is important.

> Carol Andrews,
> Macabre Daydreams

I find a lot of humor in it. If I took criticism personally, I would have drowned myself in Jim Beam years ago.

> Dark Vomit (Kelly Hutchison),
> The Vomitorium

Everything should be made fun of.

> Molly Lou McIntosh,
> Oh Boy! Cat Toy

I'm from the school of "there are no wrong answers" when it comes to creativity. Sometimes a wave of creativity leads to something really ugly, and that should be OK.

Emily O'Chiu, Candy Calamity

I appreciate something well crafted and unique, although since I found Regretsy, I also have a deep and profound appreciation for bizarre rubbish.

Amy Liebenberg, amy gillian

I think it is a part of human nature to criticize and make fun of, but it just depends on what you want to do with your energy, I guess. I can't say I've never made fun of anything, but I also love to notice the beauty in things that I don't understand.

Efia Pearson, EfiaFair

Everyone is entitled to their opinion. Even if it's wrong.

Fizaa Dosani,
BIG FIZZ House of Camp & Kitsch

sellers guide and statements

p. 4: Jodi Bloom—So Charmed (www.socharmed.etsy.com)
Jodi Bloom, designer and storyteller, is the provocateur behind So Charmed and considers herself beyond lucky to have found a productive and (relatively unless she has a power drill in her hands) safe way to focus her insane nonstop creative energy in the pursuit of glamorous and dangerous jewelry for these glamorous and dangerous times.

p. 8: Isabella Ng and Mark Beasley—"hi,billy" (www.hibilly.etsy.com)
Found objects are always romantic. They are a conversation, a calendar, a piece of sky, and a beautiful picnic day.

p. 9: Lynn Cyr—Lynn Cyr Art (www.lynncyrart.etsy.com)
Award-winning painter with collectors throughout the world. I've recently been inspired by the natural elements surrounding me, which is how my birch purses were born.

p. 10: Leanne Angwin—StudioLeanne (www.studioleanne.etsy.com)
Outrageous oversize glass and ceramic cocktail rings handmade by the artist in Melbourne, Australia. Each piece of wearable art is one of a kind.

p. 11: Efia Pearson—EfiaFair (www.efiafair.etsy.com)
My mission as an artist is to encourage inspiration. I wouldn't be in this book if I hadn't found Etsy first. I love the journey.

p. 12: Lisa Smith-Sittniewski—Alterity Button Jewelry and Gifts (www .alterity.etsy.com)

Victorian- and retro-style jewelry and gifts featuring antique and vintage buttons on Etsy and off (www.alteritybuttonjewelry.com). Most selections are serious, but many are fun!

p. 13: Bek Caruso—CleverGirl (www.clevergirl.etsy.com)
Clever. Quirky. Bold. Entrancing jewelry and unique modern classic treasures. Heirloom quality artisan direct handmade goods and world renowned personal service.

p. 14: Michael Quinn—Glampire Design (www.glampiredesign.etsy.com)
Glampire Design [GLAM-pahyuhr di-ZAHYN] Noun: 1. small business that creates one-of-a-kind accessories. Synonyms: 1. captivating, glamorous, dramatic, playful, fun, fanciful, elegant, outrageous, quirky, exceptional.

p. 15: Justine S.—JustineJustine (www.justinejustine.etsy.com)
JustineJustine is telling you an international story about jeweldesigner Justine, who makes funky jewelry with an exotic touch by using and reusing interesting materials.

p. 16: donna Valentine—Valentine Fiber Arts (www.valentinefiberarts.etsy .com)
I like to create all kinds of things. My shop is filled with ever-changing items, from pincushions to Japanese flowers to "Poor Butterflies."

pp. 17, 95: Cybele—Cybelesque (www.cybelesque.etsy.com)
My quest is to creatively and cleverly convolute quotidian components and be compensated comfortably for each contrivance I contrive to construct. I also adore alliterating.

p: 18: Nikki Ty-Tomkins—No Regretsy (www.noregretsy.etsy.com)
I've always felt the best prank provokes some doubt as to whether it really *is* a prank. "Is that for real?" is the perfect response.

p. 19: Kelly M. Sapp—Kelly's Keychains (www.egyptianruin.etsy.com)
There is nothing more fun than entertaining my inner child every day of the year. Thanks to everyone who helps me realize my dreams.

pp. 20, 128: Sara E. Lynch—Ducks and Chicks and Geese Better Scurry (www.potsdamelf.etsy.com)
Basically if I didn't make art I would end up on that show *Hoarders*. Actually I just might anyway, so please stop by my shop!

p. 21: Tina Summers—Cowgirl Heaven (www.cowgirlheaven.etsy.com)
If you can see it you can always achieve it. Remember it's your destiny, so don't stop till you reach the stars. Smile awhile.

p. 22: Heather M. Hopp—Heather's Feathers and Fluff (www.birdhopp .etsy.com)
Think Vargas girls meet Mark Ryden surreal. Headbands and clips in feathery flowery fun styles like pin-up and retro. Odd inspired unique pieces on occasion.

p. 23: Elena Siff—Elena Mary (www.elenamary.etsy.com)
As a dedicated assemblage maker, I use everything to make art—e.g., twigs. My favorite art movement: Arte Povera. Lots of Regretsy-type art there.

pp. 25, 31, 33, 35: Patti Notestine—Furbabies Boutique (www.furbabies boutique.etsy.com)
Handmade clothing and accessories to pamper your pet.

p. 30: Jennifer Grant—Goose On The Loose Jewelry (www.gooseonthe loose.etsy.com)
Goose On The Loose Jewelry features painstakingly created wearable treasures. Each original, highly detailed piece is handmade using simple tools and the highest quality materials.

p. 32: John Henderson—RoyRoadFishCompany (www.royroadfish company.etsy.com
This hat lets you hear the sounds they make, feel the air moved by their wings. It puts you in the middle of the action!

pp. 34, 51: Molly Lou McIntosh—Oh Boy! Cat Toy (www.ohboycattoy .etsy.com)
Weird Cat Toys for Weird Cats. Vegan, eco-friendly fabrics. Organic catnip

grown in America. Handmade with love and care. Custom orders welcome.

p. 37: Marc Willwerth—Perfect Children (www.PerfectChildren.etsy.com)
Perfect Children are born of postconsumer waste, love, and eyeballs. Part mythic, part mutant, and 100 percent adorable. Perfect Children for a less than perfect world.

p. 42: Kym Joseph—Crafty is the new black (www.craftyisthenewblack .etsy.com)
Specializing in Boo-Boo Monsters for GROWN-UP boo-boos, custom Felt-Me likeness dolls for the narcissist in us all, and other random works of handmade awesomeness.

p. 43: Cheryl DeWolfe—Cheryl's Creative Miscellany (www.victriviaqueen .etsy.com)
Even screwed-up robots and monsters need homes; why not buy one to make your other plush toys feel better about themselves?

p. 44: Bastet2329—Creepy Dolls (www.creepydolls.etsy.com)
Dolls are creepy anyway, I just add to that.

p. 45: Peggy Costa—Red Butted Red Heel Sock Monkey Dolls and Cards (www.atomicgrandma.etsy.com)
Made my first sock monkey in 1978. I'm still birthing sock monkeys for my grandkids and others. Plain or insane, they make people smile :(])

p. 46: Ken Henson—Planet Fugly (www.planetfugly.etsy.com)
They are watching us. Buy talismans that will interfere with their transmissions.

p. 47: Alison Bancroft—FruteJuce (www.frutejuce.etsy.com)
I submitted my chainsaw baby vest to Regretsy, but they chose the floppy bunny. No accounting for taste!

p. 48: Kathleen Paquette—MyCrafts R 4U (www.mycraftsr4u.etsy.com)
Don't belive in aliens? Then MyCrafts R not 4U.

p. 49: Coy Powers—CR Powers' Oddities, Marvels & Curiosity Candles (www.coypowers.etsy.com)
My shop isn't just art dolls and grim reapers. It's also jar babies, eyeball candles, and paintings (even cute ones!). Sideshows, steampunks, and mad scientists welcome!

p. 50: Jana Krippner—Sillycut (www.sillycut.etsy.com)
Dark adornments and more: accessories and uncommon plush creatures such as the Lolita Cat! Like to accessorize with extraordinary things? Peek for the German artist Sillycut.

pp. 56, 65: Ashleigh Heather Russell—tangerined (www.tangerined.etsy.com)
I like to highlight the humor as well as the beauty in the human form.

p. 57: Rachel Bowen—Art Harpy (www.artharpy.etsy.com)
Art Harpy, where art and mischief collide. Fabric vaginas, snarky jewelry, whimsical collage, and whatever the hell else I feel like making.

p. 58: Sharon Coleman—CozyColeman (www.cozycoleman.etsy.com)
It's easy for me to laugh at this knowing that I've made a lot of money selling this doll and pattern to midwives and doulas.

p. 59: Lisa Currie—Goodness by ArchDiva (www.archdiva.etsy.com)
Look good while doing good with Goodness by ArchDiva. Handmade beaded and sterling silver jewelry—like Vulva No. 3—with proceeds donated to charity!

p. 60: Hope Walston—Mimi's Dream (www.etsy.com/shop/Mimisdreams)
Making periods a little more entertaining, one pad at a time!

p. 61: April Munson—lumiknits (www.lumiknits.etsy.com)

p. 63: Rayna Fahey—Radical Rags (www.radicalrags.etsy.com)
Primarily a revolutionary artist and pattern designer, Rayna Fahey also uses her Etsy store as a venue to peddle unique items made from unwanted materials.

p. 64: Michael Phipps—Scatterbrain Tees (www.phippsart.etsy.com)
I've long been a fan of artsy T-shirts, so it was natural for me to start turning heads with my own line of "wearable art."

p. 66: Stacey Gordon—staceyrebecca (www.staceyrebecca.etsy.com)
I've been making warped puppets and writing warped puppet shows since 2002. I like it. Please don't tell my family.

p. 67: Emily Balivet—The Art of Emily Balivet (www.emilybalivet.etsy.com)
Emily Balivet is a entirely self-taught artist whose paintings explore the mystical feminine elements of ancient goddess mythologies from around the world.

p. 69: Claire Chambers—Absolutely Small (www.absolutelysmall.etsy.com)
Absolutely Small is Claire Chambers. Claire Chambers is a crazy-pants artist/crafter who spends most of her time indoors in Northern California. She likes making people laugh, chickens and pugs, and writing about herself in the third person.

p. 74: Eric Masters—IMOTIME (www.imotime.etsy.com)
Sometimes you see yourself better in the light of others' comments. Sometimes you don't. Sometimes it is better to just buy a damned clock already!

p. 75: Ani Ostendorff (www.aostendorff.etsy.com)
My work is a combination of ultra care/attention to detail, ridiculous fun, and versatility of use. I try to keep it flexible.

p. 76: Woody Blue—Woody Blue Rainbow Flags (www.woodybluerainbow flag.etsy.com)
Wave a flag that celebrates your passion, your ideals, your beliefs. Flags are made from recycled material. Handheld to parade-size banners. Customized orders available.

p. 77: Erin Rahel—frenzy! (www.frenzyfinds.etsy.com)
i know i can't possibly be the only person in the world who wants to cuddle with john wayne gacy at night, can i???

p. 78: Fizaa Dosani—BIG FIZZ House of Camp & Kitsch (www.bigfizz
.etsy.com)
If it's got a head, I can mount it. Warning: Sensitive plush-toy lovers must
proceed with caution.

p. 79: Lauren Marsella—Free Lauren Marsella (www.freelaurenmarsella
.etsy.com)
She is the greatest unknown, living American artist. You're not listening!
You're just tweezing your belly-button hairs!

p. 80: Amy Liebenberg—amy gillian (www.amygillian.etsy.com)
Amy spends all her time doing the following things: etching, drawing,
knitting, using natural dyes, weaving, pottery, sewing, painting, photography, printing, spinning fiber, adventuring, and dreaming.

p. 81: Emily O'Chiu—Candy Calamity (www.candycalamity.etsy.com)
Candy Calamity is handmade recycled art and jewelry inspired by candy
wrappers, packaging, bright-colored tissue, repurposed fabrics, and other
fun recyclables.

p. 82: Garrick Weber—Boxes 'N' More (www.boxnmor.etsy.com)

p. 83: Sarah Singleton—Whitewash Sundries (www.whitewashsundries
.etsy.com)
It's funny that my vampire wineglasses were featured on Regretsy, and
even funnier if anyone took them more seriously than what they were intended to be: a unique conversation piece.

p. 85: Denny Pinkham (www.pinky27889.etsy.com)
I'm Denny Pinkham, the folk painter with a pop art mentality. Painting
bars, beaches, good tunes, and social commentary, whether you like it
or not.

p. 90: Brooks Werner—Hautestew (www.hautestew.etsy.com)
My goal as an artist is to make people say "What!?" at any chance. That's
why I think myself and Regretsy are a perfect match!

p. 91: Carol Andrews—Macabre Daydreams (www.cobaltmoonchild.etsy
.com)
I am grateful for the opportunity to share my artistic vision with the
world. I aim to stir emotion from my audience with my work.

pp. 92, 94, 97: CappySue—Cappy Sue Creations (www.cappysue.etsy.com)
I paint wild vivid dreams I have every night each day. I feel very lucky.
Thank you, Josh, Cindy, and Dad for encouraging my work.

p. 93: Raven Young—Dreadful Things By Raven (www.ravenofskys.etsy
.com)
Dreadful Things By Raven is a macabre carnival of the bizarre. Raven
Young's paintings feature subject matter such as roadkill and she sells real
skull/bone jewelry.

p. 96: Kyley Quinn—Latebloomers Art (www.latebloomers328.etsy.com)
Indie Rock Kid Art.

p. 98: Sabrina Zbasnik—Introverted Painting (www.blablover5.etsy.com)
For all your invisible bride and groom painting needs, visit Introverted
Painting. I'll even throw in a beach, dog, or radioactive monster for free.

p. 99: Kelly Hutchison—The Vomitorium (www.darkvomit.etsy.com)
F#%king Flies "poop on my fresh oil paintings drying . . . and then they
screw."

p. 100: Kristi McMurry—Kristi McMurry Photography Prints and Greet-
ing Cards (www.kristimcmurry.etsy.com)
I'm a big fan of humor, silliness, and irony. I think that might have something to do with the photographs I take.

p. 101: Krista Allison—canoo (www.canoo.etsy.com)
Krista Allison devotes an inordinate amount of time to proper word
choice, you nosy bastard. Now get off my lawn before I call the cops.

p. 106: Teena Schorr—SoapyHo (www.soapyho.com)
On my webite you will find adult soaps as well as funny corn poo soap!
Teddy bears having sex and picture soaps will amaze you!

p. 107: Morgan Fields—SlightlyCurious (www.slightlycurious.etsy.com)
Who doesn't need a little curiosity in their life? There's enough strange taxidermy for everyone to get their claws on. Hey, no pinching!

p. 108: Aram Homampour (www.goldclip.net)
I love creating, art, clips, joy. I am an artist who loves. I create. For me that is all there is, to create and appreciate.

p. 109: Kim Greene—Kim's Classy Commodes (www.kimsclassycommodes
.etsy.com)
Is it time to redo your bathroom without a complete makeover? Here's your opportunity without breaking the bank.

p. 110: Sheryl Westleigh—Noadi's Art (www.noadi.etsy.com)
Polymer clay jewelry creations and mixed-media sculptures inspired by a love of marine animals, science, and all things weird and wonderful.

p. 111: Jennifer Laske-Cook—jr soaps (www.halflyng.etsy.com)
Halflyng started as a hobby, turned into a business, and is now being sold to help my thirty-year-old cousin, who recently had a stroke.

p. 112: Ann-Marie MacKay—the chicks with sticks (www.sprouty25.etsy
.com)
I am SAHM who is obsessed with knitting, spinning yarn, dyeing fibers, and making soap. Everyone loves bacon—now you can have bacon soap!

p. 113: Jennifer Talley—The Naughty Hook (www.naughtyhook.etsy.com)
Jen taught herself to crochet in 2002 and made her first Chapstick cozy on a flight to Newark in 2008. Her seatmate was not amused.

pp. 114, 119: Robin Crider—HiBird (www.hibird.etsy.com)
People say, "Why?" HiBird says, "Why not? The thrill comes from the smiles and giggles, knowing that just for a moment someone forgot their trials. Smile!"

p. 115: Cathy Lybarger—Aardvark Art Glass (www.aardvarkartglass.etsy
.com)

Zany handmade lampworked glass beads: creatures, abstract faces and more. Great for beaded projects and just looking at or talking to—whatever helps!

p. 116: Caroline Moore—Sixhours Photography (www.sixhours.etsy.com)
I'm a photographer, illustrator, designer, and all-around Web geek who lives in Maine with my husband, Tim, and our daughter, Elspeth.

p. 117: Kevin Stevens and Tori Carpenter—Fairy Furnishings (www.fairy furnishings.etsy.com)
We specialize in fairy furniture for collectors of all ages. All items are handcrafted in our magical woodland studio using forest bits and fairy dust (acquired long ago).

pp. 124, 125: Elaine Gladney and Billie Balizet—The Worst Shop Ever (www.theworstshopever.etsy.com)
Two cousins from southern Colorado who have been inspired by Regretsy to bring crappy creations and tacky vintage finds to the Etsy marketplace.

p. 126: Heather Leavers—Niftyknits (www.niftyknits.etsy.com)
Niftyknits, designed and handknitted in the U.K. by Heather: costumed meerkats a speciality! Commissions always welcome. You name it, I'll knit it!

p. 127: Waxela Sananda—SpiritMama (www.spiritmama.etsy.com)
I'm an artist, mom, wife, thinker, and lover of creativity. I enjoy creating art that inspires people to laugh, sing, snort, shout, or be speechless.

photo credits

Page 50: Jana Krippner

Page 51: Molly Lou McIntosh

Page 56: Ashleigh Heather Russell

Page 57: Rachel Bowen

Page 58: Sharon Coleman

Page 59: Lisa Currie

Page 60: Hope Walston

Page 61: April Munson

Page 62: Karina Nathan

Page 63: Rayna Fahey

Page 64: Michael Phipps

Page 65: Ashleigh Heather Russell

Page 66: Stacey Gordon

Page 67: Emily Balivet

Page 69: Claire Chambers

Page 74: Eric Masters

Page 75: Ani Ostendorff

Page 76: Woody Blue

Page 77: Erin Rahel

Page 78: Fizaa Dosani

Page 79: Lauren Marsella

Page 80: Amy Liebenberg

Page 81: Emily O'Chiu

Page 82: Garrick Weber

Page 83: Sarah Singleton

Page 85: Denny Pinkham

Page 90: Brooks Werner

Page 91: Carol Andrews

Page 92: CappySue

Page 93: Raven Young

Page 94: CappySue

Page 95: Cybele

Page 96: Kyley Quinn

Page 97: CappySue

Page 98: Sabrina Zbasnik

Page 99: Kelly Hutchison

Page 100: Kristi McMurry

Page 101: Krista Allison

Page 106: Teena Schorr

Page 107: Morgan Fields

Page 108: Aram Homampour

Page 109: Kim Greene

Page 110: Sheryl Westleigh

Page 111: Jennifer Laske-Cook

Page 112: Ann-Marie MacKay

Page 113: Jennifer Talley

Page 114: Robin Crider

Page 115: Cathy Lybarger

Page 116: Caroline Moore

Page 117: Kevin Stevens and Tori Carpenter

Page 119: Robin Crider

Page 124: Elaine Gladney and Billie Balizet

Page 125: Elaine Gladney and Billie Balizet

Page 126: Heather Leavers

Page 127: Waxela Sananda

Page 128: Sara E. Lynch

According to *Los Angeles* magazine, APRIL WINCHELL is the twenty-first funniest person in L.A. (which is apparently funnier than Eddie Izzard, but not quite as hilarious as Johnny Knoxville). She has enjoyed a multifaceted career in the entertainment business, owing in large part to her extremely limited attention span. She has hosted her own popular talk radio show, written for the classic sitcom *Roseanne,* voiced hundreds of animated movies and television programs (her father, the late Paul Winchell, was the original voice of Tigger), and, as a copywriter and producer, has won every major advertising award in the world. Even though she has been writing professionally since 1989, she still finds talking about herself in the third person really uncomfortable.